CREATIVE TRAINING TECHNIQUES HANDBOOK

SECOND EDITION

TIPS, TACTICS, AND HOW-TO'S FOR DELIVERING EFFECTIVE TRAINING

BY ROBERT W. PIKE, CSP

QUANTITY SALES

Most Lakewood books are available at special quantity discounts when purchased in bulk by companies, organizations, and special-interest groups. Custom imprinting or excerpting can also be done to fit special needs. For details write: Lakewood Books, 50 South Ninth Street, Minneapolis, MN 55402 or call (612) 333-0471, (800) 707-7769.

LAKEWOOD BOOKS
50 South Ninth Street
Minneapolis, MN 55402
(612) 333-0471, (800) 707-7769

Creative Training Techniques Handbook, Second Edition
Tips, Tactics, and How-To's For Delivering Effective Training
By Robert W. Pike, CSP

Publisher: Philip Jones
Editorial Coordinator: Becky Wilkinson
Copy Editor: Becky Wilkinson
Production Editor: Susan Abbott
Designer: Lecy Design

With special thanks to: Becky Wilkinson, Carol Swanson, Pat Grawert, Susan Abbott, and Lecy Design

10

Lakewood Publications Inc. publishes TRAINING Magazine, Training Director's Forum Newsletter, Creative Training Techniques Newsletter, Technology for Learning Newsletter, Potentials In Marketing Magazine, Presentations magazine, and other business periodicals and books. James P. Secord, president; Mary Hanson, Philip G. Jones, Linda Klemstein, Bryan Powell, Jerry C. Noack, Mike Murrell, vice presidents.

ISBN 0-943210-33-X (hard cover)

TABLE OF CONTENTS

PREFACE/*Philip Jones*

PREFACE

A participant in one of Bob Pike's Creative Training Techniques workshops once asked on a post-workshop card, "Can you please make some clones of this guy?" His request wasn't unusual—and it's one reason why this book was probably inevitable.

For over a decade, Pike has been one of the most popular and sought-after speakers on the HRD circuit. Creative Training Techniques (CTT), a remarkable system of ideas, techniques, strategies, tactics, and tips for anyone who wants to train or give presentations with maximum effectiveness, is why. This book is an expanded and revised second edition of the handbook Pike developed for Creative Training Techniques participants. It's intended both for CTT graduates and for those who have never heard of Pike or his system. It recreates the Creative Training Techniques process in a way that's stimulating, easy to understand, and so practical you'll start putting some of Pike's ideas to work *tomorrow*. That's almost guaranteed.

To understand CTT, you need to understand a few things about Bob Pike. After an achievement-filled adolescence followed by a Congressional appointment to the U.S. Naval Academy, Pike did a surprising about-face and entered the Moody Bible Institute in Chicago. His goal was to be a preacher. Later, after being pastor at a small evangelical church and discovering that preaching couldn't pay the rent, Pike wandered into training —first, as a salesman and trainer for a Denver-based training company and, eventually, as one of the company's top marketing executives, product developers, and presenters.

Over the next decade, Bob Pike's "style" began to take shape. That style combined Pike's instinctive ability to inspire and motivate people (not surprising from a preacher turned salesman), an increasingly sophisticated grasp of adult-learning theories and techniques, and, maybe most important, a deep belief in the inherent abilities of people to control their own destinies and development—in other words, their essential "goodness," a term I don't think Pike would object to. By 1980, when Pike formed his own business, he was on his way to being a "master" trainer. His training activities since then have spanned the HRD gamut, but at the core of Pike's special appeal was what he called Creative Training Techniques. Over the last several years in presentations before scores of groups, Creative Training Techniques became a bona fide phenomenon—thanks partly to Pike's indefatigable energy (a marathon runner, Pike is on the road giving presentations hundreds of days a year) and mostly to the special appeal of his message.

Creative Training Techniques aims to create a comprehensive conceptual and practical framework for generating learning results through participant discovery and involvement. It gives trainers the power to unleash the inherent learning potential of adults. By making learning enjoyable, it encourages participants to keep learning long after the training session. By all accounts, it succeeds. With CTT, training becomes more productive, more satisfying, more fun. Many of the elements of CTT aren't necessarily original or unique, but few (if any) HRD professionals have Pike's ability to synthesize so many ideas into such an easy-to-follow, commonsensical and, at the same time, insightful set of training tools. Pike dips effortlessly into philosophy, psychology, technology, and other weighty areas to explore the elements of adult-learner perception, motivation, and retention. At the same time, he discusses such seemingly simple topics as seating arrangements, flip charts, overhead transparencies, magic markers, and so on. And, as he shuttles back and forth between concept and practice, the CTT "process" begins to take shape. Pike includes plenty of techniques to keep the process fresh in your mind and ready when you need it. Thanks to CTT, no one we can think of, in a field crowded with rivals, has been as successful as Bob Pike in helping people become effective trainers.

How successful? Over 50,000 people internationally have attended a CTT seminar as of this writing, and hundreds of companies have sponsored CTT seminars. Walt Disney World, Citibank, IBM, AT&T, Shell, American Express, and others have incorporated Pike's ideas and techniques into their in-house train-the-trainer programs. The *Creative Training Techniques Newsletter,* a short monthly roundup of training tips, tactics, and ideas edited by Pike, attracted 6,000 subscribers in its first year alone. And when Pike appears before groups of trainers at conferences and professional events, it's virtually always standing room only.

Later in this book, you'll come across this passage: "Our purpose as trainers is not primarily to counsel, interpret, instruct, or in any way lead people to believe that we are to supply the answers to their questions. Instead, we should let the seminar, the instruments, the projects, the case studies, and other materials serve as resources that the participants can draw on to solve their problems and develop appropriate plans of action.... The approach I recommend limits lecture and maximizes discovery and participation. Sometimes, it may not seem as if you're needed, but you are—often in ways the participants don't perceive. Ideally, you're the best kind of teacher—a facilitator of insight, change, and growth who teaches that answers come from within. Your personal attitudes and your role modeling will set the tone for your participants. And your seriousness of purpose, your personal planning, and your adherence to the guidelines you establish, along with your interest and enthusiasm for both the content and the participants, will facilitate change and learning for your participants."

Such an approach requires—both for you as a trainer and presenter and for participants—some adjustments from the old teacher-centered way of doing things. Bob Pike's special gift is showing you how to make those adjustments easily and effectively. We're pleased and proud to be able bring the second edition of *The Creative Training Techniques Handbook* to you. We think you'll find it indispensable.

Philip Jones

Lakewood Publications

ACKNOWLEDGMENTS
for the Second Edition

Creative Training Techniques continues to be more widely used. More than 50,000 trainers on five continents have now taken the two day program. More than 65,000 now have the first edition of the handbook to use as a guide to their training and development efforts. Their implementation of Creative Training Techniques and subsequent feedback have enabled us to produce this second edition.

As with the first edition of *The Creative Training Techniques Handbook*, I would like to acknowledge those who merit special recognition, both in their contributions to this book, and in their contributions to Creative Training Techniques.

Creative Training Techniques trainers/consultants who continue to do an outstanding job of delivering more than 220 public two day programs per year in addition to more than 100 in-house programs. Lynn Solem and Doug McCallum continue to set a high standard for excellence along with Michele Deck, Lori Backer, Tim Richardson, and Rich Ragan. They have also provided generous support to the six new trainers who will be joining us.

Rich Meiss, vice president of development for Creative Training Techniques. We have worked together in several organizations for longer than either of us wants to admit. We could not maintain growth with quality without his work with the trainers, consultants, and marketing staff.

The support staff at Resources for Organizations, Inc. (ROI): especially Sandi Dufault who updated all the references for this edition.

The staff of Lakewood Publications: especially Philip G. Jones, vice president; Becky Wilkinson who coordinated everything needed to make this second edition happen, including countless hours of proofreading; Carol Swanson, who coordinated the redesign of the cover; and Susan Abbott, who put in a great deal of time and effort reformatting the new edition, revamping the existing graphics, as well as producing the new ones.

And finally, and again most importantly, Audrey Roholt, vice president of Resources for Organizations, Inc. Everything I said in the first edition acknowledgments is still true today. After ten years of working together she remains a trusted friend and advisor as well as valued colleague.

ACKNOWLEDGMENTS
for the First Edition

Many individuals deserve credit for their contributions to the first edition of *The Creative Training Techniques Handbook*. I would like to acknowledge those who merit special recognition.

Diane McInerny, who was my partner in Communication Consultants.

Lynn Solem, Doug McCallum, and Jonathan Odell, whose talents in leading the Creative Training Techniques seminar have greatly increased our ability to meet the needs of trainers.

The support staff at Resources for Organizations, Inc. (ROI): Sandi Dufault, whose mastery of desktop publishing continues to improve all the training materials we produce; Pam Zubrod, for making sure all the seminars are set up properly and run smoothly; and Julie Faust, our Little Miss Everything, who follows through like no one else.

The staff at Lakewood Publications: Philip G. Jones, vice president of Lakewood, who saw the potential for this book and put the team together to make it happen; Susan C. Jones, whose editing skills made the book much more clear and useful than it would have been otherwise; Brian McDermott, who, as editorial director of *Creative Training Techniques Newsletter,* has challenged me to express myself more clearly in print and whose practical orientation has served me very well; Julie Swiler, who has patiently coordinated every aspect of this book, asked me hundreds of clarifying questions, and tracked me down all over the globe. The quality of this book is a direct reflection of Julie's unflagging efforts.

And, finally, and most importantly, Audrey Roholt, vice president of Resources for Organizations, Inc., whose loyalty and commitment to the vision have demonstrated themselves in the form of careful attention to all the details that are required for an organization to meet the needs of its clients with excellence.

CREATIVE TRAINING TECHNIQUES

For more than twenty years, Robert W. Pike and his colleagues have been developing and presenting seminars, workshops and training programs throughout the world.

Year after year, trainers, consultants, managers and senior executives have asked:

- "How can we get more out of our training efforts?"
- "Our training is routine—how can we make it exciting?"
- "Results! Help us get the results we need—and fast!"

Creative Training Techniques is a practical, results-guaranteed solution to your training needs. More than 50,000 persons have attended this intensive two-day workshop, offered more than 200 times around the world each year.

ADDITIONAL SEMINAR AND TRAINING PROGRAMS OFFERED BY ROI

Resources for Organizations Incorporated has developed and presented more than 37 different management development, sales training, organizational and personal development programs and seminars. Our audiences range from Fortune 500 corporate leadership teams to entrepreneurial start-ups, from members of various professional and management associations to university faculties, and others.

CONSULTING SERVICES

Bob Pike and all our senior consultants are available for individual consulting, design and training engagements.

TRAINING AND DEVELOPMENT MATERIALS THAT ARE ALMOST IMPOSSIBLE TO FIND

Because of our commitment to serving all of your training and development needs, Resources for Organizations Incorporated is your source for hard-to-find training and presentation aids. While we always direct you to local suppliers whenever possible, some very useful items are nearly impossible to find. We "scout the world" for useful products and make them available to you.

CAN WE PROVIDE YOU WITH MORE INFORMATION?

Call us at (612) 829-1954, send a fax to (612) 829-0260
or write to us at:
Resources for Organizations Incorporated
7620 West 78th Street
Edina, Minnesota 55439

ABOUT THE AUTHOR

Robert W. Pike is a highly acclaimed speaker, master trainer, and consultant in the human resources development field. He has developed and implemented training programs for business, industry, and government since 1969. As president of the Minnesota-based Resources for Organizations and Creative Training Techniques International, Inc., Pike has worked with dozens of major corporations, including IBM, AT&T, NASA, Pfizer, Upjohn, Walt Disney World, and many others. His Creative Training Techniques workshop has been delivered to over 50,000 HRD professionals. Pike also has been a featured speaker at national and regional conferences for the American Society for Training and Development and other professional organizations and has appeared as an HRD master at *TRAINING* Magazine conferences. One of the most popular HRD presenters today, Pike has instructed and inspired thousands of trainers on sales, marketing, leadership, attitudes, motivation, and personal development and purpose.

Pike is the author of numerous articles and three books and is editor of *Creative Training Techniques* Newsletter. He attended the U.S. Naval Academy and received a divinity degree from the Moody Bible Institute in Chicago. He has six children and lives in Minneapolis. Pike's hobbies include downhill skiing, scuba diving, and running.

CREATIVE GENESIS

1

The Origin and Foundation of
Creative Training Techniques

Creative Training Techniques are instructor-led, participant-centered training concepts. Training, as much as possible, should be a do-it-yourself project for the participants involved. But I didn't realize that when I began my career in 1969 selling and delivering sales-training and management-development programs. I was, if I may say so, an effective presenter. Twice a week, I would conduct seminars, and I always received among the highest ratings of any of the presenters, even those with significantly more experience. At just 22, I felt I had arrived as a trainer; in retrospect, I see that I was essentially an effective presenter or speaker. When you're the only one who knows anything about a particular subject and you're giving presentations that last a couple of hours or even a whole day, being an effective presenter is important. But it doesn't necessarily mean you know how to deliver training.

The purpose of any training program is to deliver results. People must be more effective after the training than they were before. What do they now know that they didn't before? What can they now do that they couldn't? How have their feelings and attitudes changed and/or improved as a result? If change hasn't taken place that benefits the individual and the organization, I'm not really sure that training has been delivered.

Three years after my career began, I had developed a variety of training programs for internal use that ranged in length from two hours to three weeks. I learned to break people into groups and to give them hands-on opportunities to apply the content being covered. Yet I continued to rely upon a lecture format.

That changed in 1973, when I traveled to Minneapolis to evaluate a seminar I was considering adding to my business. Called "Adventures in Attitudes," it was a 30-hour course in human relations, communications, problem solving, interpersonal skills, and self-management. The first day, 30 of us gathered in a room and were seated in groups of five. The instructor made a few brief introductory remarks and then passed out written materials for each group to discuss. After each group summarized its discussions, we moved on to the next activity. When it was time for a lecture, the instructor would play an audiotape. By noon, I was still waiting for him to say something so I could evaluate the quality of the program. I was still waiting at the end of the first day.

The second day continued in much the same vein. I kept waiting. I finally decided that, if the time and money I had invested were going to be worth something, it was going to be because of me. I wasn't going to get it from the instructor.

Finally, on the third day, it hit me like a ton of bricks: I realized I could recall almost all our discussions and activities *because I had been involved*. I had made some significant discoveries and decisions—and I had truly learned—because I had truly participated.

I consider that experience to be my first, and most significant, contact with training that is based on discovery, participation, and involvement. I returned to Denver, and, in the last four months of 1973, I did 10 percent of the company's volume. In 1974, I moved from Denver to Minneapolis and became vice-president of Personal Dynamics. Over the next six years, enrollments in the program grew from 4,000 per year to over 80,000 per year. Today, 20 years later, I have clients, such as American Express, Southwestern Bell, and Nationwide Insurance, that continue to use the program to make a difference in their organizations.

In 1980, I decided to go out on my own. I started by developing a course on team building and conflict management, and I found the principles of learner-discovery, participation, and involvement worked there. Next, I designed and delivered a program on problem solving and decision making, and the techniques based on those principles worked there, too.

In 1981, I conducted a three-hour seminar on the techniques themselves for a local chapter of the American Society for Training and Development (ASTD). I reasoned that, if I was designing do-it-yourself training, trainers I worked with should also be applying the principles as a do-it-yourself project. That's what the seminar was all about, and it was an unqualified success.

I presented these ideas to a national audience for the first time in 1982 at the ASTD national conference. Three hundred people crowded into a room designed for 160, and more than 100 others were turned away. At every ASTD conference since then, in more than 40 ASTD chapters, at more than a dozen ASTD regional conferences, at every conference *TRAINING* Magazine has sponsored since 1980, I've presented the concept, and the response has been overwhelmingly positive. Furthermore, the concept seems to be global: audiences representing more than 50 countries have been excited about the ideas when I've presented them at conferences in Europe, Japan, and the Middle East.

As soon as people learned about Creative Training Techniques, they asked where they could get more information on the subject, but I didn't know where to direct them. I had read and researched, but the most I could find were snippets here and there. So I wrote a manual on Creative Training Techniques that has formed the foundation for this book, which is a greatly revised and expanded version. Since 1981, 50,000 trainers have been through a one-day or longer version of Creative Training Techniques. I hope that, by the time you finish this book, Creative Training Techniques will seem as eminently practical and applicable to you as they have proved to be for me.

SOME FOUNDATION PRINCIPLES

A lot of different threads run through Creative Training Techniques. I've devised what I call "Pike's Laws of Adult Learning." These, along with an aphorism from Confucius, are the foundation principles underlying Creative Training Techniques—and this book.

Law 1. Adults Are Babies with Big Bodies

Recall the kinds of learning activities we did as small children. In kindergarten, we colored, drew, played games, modeled with clay, fingerpainted, etc.—all hands-on activities. Children with very little experience learn through experience.

When we reached first, second, and third grade, we lined up in rows, and we were talked *at*. Rarely were we encouraged, or even permitted, to be involved in the learning process. The more experience we had, the less that experience was used. As adults, we bring a lot of experience to our training programs. We want to acknowledge, honor, and celebrate that experience. If, as children with very little experience, we could discover and learn, how much more as adults can we discover and learn.

Law 2. People Don't Argue with Their Own Data

If I say something is true, you might say to yourself, "He's got to believe it; he's teaching it." But if you say it, for you it's true.

For example, through research we might identify 15 characteristics of an effective leader. But rather than pre-

3

senting them, I might choose to have small groups discuss the most effective leaders they've ever known and identify the characteristics that made those leaders effective. Normally, the groups will come up with 80 percent of the characteristics. It's easy for the instructor to fill in the other 20 percent. And I find the group much more willing to accept my suggestions for that remaining 20 percent than if I try to present all of them.

That's why I also compile action-idea lists in my seminars. I ask participants to look for ideas, concepts, and techniques for which they see an immediate use back on their jobs. From time to time, I'll ask volunteers to share the ideas they've picked up. It reinforces the value of the training and demonstrates, again, that people don't argue with their own data. Whether it's a technical course, management course, or sales course, the concept works. People look for the things they can use back on the job.

Law 3. Learning Is Directly Proportional to the Amount of Fun You Have

Now I'm not necessarily referring to jokes or pointless games or entertainment. I'm referring to the sheer joy of learning that can come from involvement and participation. From realizing that you can use your own energy to learn—and enjoy learning because you're gaining information, tools, techniques, etc., that can benefit you. These acquisitions are going to help you do your job faster, better, easier, and they're going to help you solve problems.

We live in the age of entertainment. When I was growing up in Chicago in the early '50s, there were only a couple of television channels, both of them black and white. People watched one channel all evening long because there were no other options. Today it's different. Many of us have cable television and remote-control units. We turn on the TV and basically say, "You've got six seconds to grab my attention, or I'm gone." We then flip through 68 channels of cable, look at each other, and say, "There's nothing on." Years ago, we happily watched one channel all night long, but today there's nothing on! We have the same attitude toward videocassette recorders; we go to the video store, look through thousands of titles for 15 minutes, and declare, "There's nothing here."

Few of us have the entertainment skills of Bob Hope, John Cleese, Bill Cosby, or Joan Rivers. Few of us are able to keep the riveted attention of an audience for hours. Fortunately, we don't have to. We can use the energy, involvement, and participation of our audience to put into their personal learning experiences the excitement they vicariously get from some of their entertainment activities.

4

Humor itself, the kind that produces genuine, heartfelt laughter, can enhance the learning that takes place. One only has to read Norman Cousins' *Anatomy of an Illness* to realize that humor can aid enormously in reducing stress and anxiety, allowing people to relax and be more open to the learning process. That kind of humor should make a point and not simply provide amusement. Used judiciously, it should enhance the learning process and enable participants to derive greater benefit.

Law 4. *Learning Has Not Taken Place Until Behavior Has Changed*

In training, it's not what you know but what you *do* with what you know that counts. That's why skill practice is so important in our training sessions. If we want people to do things differently, we must provide them with many opportunities to be comfortable accepting new ideas in a nonthreatening environment. It's one thing to know something intellectually; it's quite another to have the emotional conviction that comes from personal experience.

C.S. Lewis, the English philosopher, said, "A man with an experience is never at the mercy of a man with an argument." Today, he probably would have said "person," but his point would be the same: Give people success experiences in using our information and techniques in whatever learning environment we have available so that we increase the likelihood of on-the-job application.

Law 5. *Fu Yu, Wu Yu, Wzu Tu Yu*

Roughly translated this means: Momma's having it or Papa's having it ain't like baby having it. If I can do something, so what? That's like Momma's having it. The fact that you, as one of my participants, can do something, so what. That's like Papa's having it. It's when you can pass what you've learned on to someone else that I, as a trainer, know I've really done my job.

This law may seem silly, but in my seminars and in this handbook I'm using that silliness to make a serious point: It doesn't matter what I can do or what I can teach you to do. Ultimately what matters is what I can teach you to teach others to do. This is one confirmation of your competence—when you can pass what you know on to someone else.

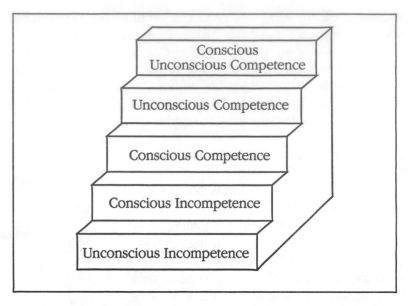

In his book *Empathic Communications*, William Howell identifies various levels of competence. They are stages we all go through in the learning process. Howell identifies four fundamental stages, and I'd like to add a fifth.

Howell's model starts at the bottom of a stairway with Level 1—Unconscious Incompetence: We're not competent, but we don't know it. Most of us, until the age of 16 or so, were unconsciously incompetent in terms of our ability to drive a car. We thought it would be a breeze to drive because our parents did it so effortlessly. How wrong we were! I'll never forget my first time behind the wheel. I put the key in the ignition, depressed the clutch, gave the car some gas, put the car in reverse, and let up on the clutch. The car shuddered to a halt. In an instant, I moved to Level 2—Conscious Incompetence. I was incompetent, and now I knew it. After a lot of practice, I arrived at Level 3—Conscious Competence. I now could drive the car, but I was always tense about my abilities—or lack of them. It was difficult to relax. Finally I arrived at Level 4—Unconscious Competence. I no longer had to think about everything that driving a car involved because the act had become automatic.

The level I'd like to add is, Level 5—Conscious Unconscious Competence. Not only are we competent and can run on autopilot, so to speak, but we also can verbalize to others the how-to's of how we're able to do what we do. Many of us can arrive quite readily at Level 4, but it's far more difficult to reach Level 5. For example, I seem to have the knack of using natural humor in my presentations. I don't tell jokes, but the real-life illustrations I use and the way I "play" off participant comments bring laughter. I haven't, however, arrived at the point where I can explain that part of what I do to someone else. I'm still at Level 4 in this department.

In some of our training, Level 4 may be just fine. But enabling people to transfer what they know to someone else without our continually needing to be the focal point of the learning process is certain to be one training target in the future. Considerable training (and retraining) will be needed, but there won't be enough "professionals" to do it. So creating awareness of Level 5 and allowing some practice at reaching that level in class will be crucial.

"What I hear,
I forget;
What I see,
I remember;
but what I do
I understand."
– Confucius, 451 B.C.

So much for "Pike's Laws of Adult Learning." Confucius, back in 451 B.C., made a sage observation that still applies today: "What I hear, I forget; what I see, I remember; but what I *do* (emphasis mine) I understand." And isn't that the purpose of training? Not simply to have participants hear nor even necessarily to remember but to apply, to do—and to do with understanding. Change based upon action and understanding invariably is change for the better.

These are the foundations of Creative Training Techniques. In the following chapters, you'll go through a cafeteria line of techniques that can help you make your training instructor-led but participant-centered. Let me suggest that you create your own action-idea list as you proceed. Just as you don't pick up all the food on the cafeteria line, neither should you try to pick up and apply every idea I offer here. Instead, look for those you can use now. Then return to the book when you're ready for "second helpings."

PRESENTATION PREPARATION

2

*How to Get Rave Reviews and Results
Before You Open Your Mouth*

I believe that 80 percent of being creative and being able to involve people in a presentation depends upon adequate preparation. Granted, some presenters like to take their expertise and simply shoot from the hip; experience tells them they can hit the target often enough to do the job. Most others, though, realize that preparation is the real key to an outstanding training program. They're the ones who accept the six Ps of an effective presentation: *Proper Preparation and Practice Prevent Poor Performance.*

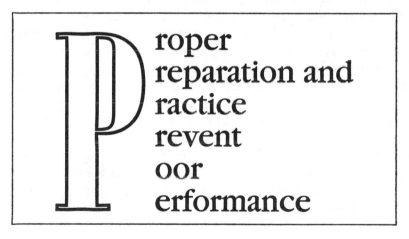

roper
reparation and
ractice
revent
oor
erformance

Preparation assures them that they'll be able to deliver what the client needs. And that's your goal too—to design and deliver training that gets results. Systematic preparation increases both the ease and the likelihood of successful training.

EIGHT STEPS TO PROPER PREPARATION

Step 1. List Your Needs, Both General and Specific

The first question I ask regarding this step is: Who says these are needs? In my experience, training should be designed for three groups of people, two of who may never show up in the classroom. One group is the senders, the managers or supervisors who are sending people to this particular training program. What are these people's needs and expectations? What is it going to take to make these people eager to support your training program? Obviously, we want their support, but if we don't consider them as we're developing the program we may not have it.

Designing training for only one person (e.g., the participant or sendee) is a little like trying to sit on a three-legged stool that has only one leg. You can do it, but it's not very comfortable.

Second, we need to design for the sendees, the actual participants. Most of the time, we're pretty good at focusing on these individuals.

Finally, we need to design for the payers, those who provide the budget. What return do they expect for their training dollar?

As we draw up a list of needs that must be met in this training program, we also have to ask, "How important is it that we meet *all* of them?" To answer this question, we should keep two things in mind. First, our needs assessment must be complete and thorough, and, second, we must have buy-in from the three groups whose support we need.

In order to encourage that buy-in, keep in mind two important baseline rules. Number one, get input from one level up and one level down when doing any needs assessment. For example, if you're designing training for supervisors, ask both the supervisors' managers for input and the supervisors' employees for input. The training target group may not clearly see its own needs.

The second baseline rule is to use *nonrepetitive redundant measures*. This means we must assess the needs in at least two different ways. If, for example, you're designing a training program for salespeople, you survey the salespeople, who might say, "Our problems concern closing and time management." The managers of those salespeople would agree: "Our salespeople seem to have problems with closing and with time management." If you don't choose to talk with the involved customers about the needs of these salespeople, you would stop at this point and conclude, "We understand the needs because the managers and the salespeople have identified them." You've used one measure—the interview method —and you've found that the two groups have the same perception. Now, let's say that you've used another measure. You've spent a day observing high-performance and low-performance salespeople and noted that both groups used their time in exactly the same way.

The only difference between high- and low-performing salespeople, then, is their approach to closing.

Nonrepetitive redundant measures provide two different methods for looking at the same information. *Nonrepetitive* means that the measure does not repeat itself. *Redundant* refers to the fact that it measures the same thing. In this example, the primary focus of your training would be on the issue that has been identified—closing. Because both the salespeople and their supervisors also have a perceived, or psychological, need for time management, you might also provide some material on this subject, but your primary focus would be on closing.

Participant support and ownership are imperative in order for Creative Training Techniques to succeed. And achieving the total involvement of trainees must be considered in completing the first step of the preparation process. The more buy-in we have, the more likely we are to get the results we want.

One strategy we have found useful is the formation of an advisory committee to review the program during its development. This committee generally consists of people whose support is key to the program's implementation and on-the-job follow-up. Committee members might be managers, subject-matter experts, performers—in other words, a representative cross section of the senders, the sendees, and the payers. You also want to consider people who will enhance the credibility of the program as it is being designed and eventually introduced.

We are looking for two things from an advisory committee: input and influence.

- *Input*—because some of the members may be experts on the subject-matter, may have a history with the organization, or may possess other valuable information.
- *Influence*—because of the respect that these members have in the organization that can loan credibility to our programs.

Step 2. Assess Your Audience
Learn all you can about your participants in terms of the following factors.

- *Knowledge*—How much knowledge and experience will participants bring to a program? Remember the adage: Never underestimate the intelligence of your listeners; never overestimate their need for information. For example, you may take for granted that most businesspeople are familiar with the concept of equipment depreciation, but don't expect them to know which depreciation formula necessarily applies to their organization or to various kinds of equipment.

• *Interest*—The success of your presentation is 50 percent assured if your audience's interest is working for you from the beginning. Every single person in the audience is going to be tuned in to radio station *WII-FM;* they're all going to be asking themselves, "What's in it for me? How will it help me do my job faster, better, easier? What losses am I going to avoid? What benefits am I going to gain?" Each of the three key groups—senders, sendees, and payers—we mentioned earlier will be tuned to this radio station. What's the pay-off if they support or are involved in this training?

We must consider two things about our audience's interest level. First, what is their level of interest coming into the program, and, second, what can we do at the beginning of the program to stimulate that interest even further? How can we develop in them a sense of anticipation for a pay-off?

One other point to remember here is that people don't argue with their own data. If somebody says something is true, it *is* true—for that person.

One way to open a training program is to ask people to brainstorm responses to two questions.

1. What kinds of problems do people have because they don't _____ (Fill in the blank with the topic of your training program, e.g., solve problems effectively, delegate effectively, follow safety procedures, know how to handle objections and put-offs, understand or use reference manuals, etc.)

2. What happens when you and I do _____ _____ (Fill in the blank with the same answers provided to the first question, e.g., solve problems effectively, delegate effectively, follow safety procedures, etc.)

You can then ask the group for their responses to these questions and post them. Or you can have participants discuss their responses to the two questions in small groups. If I have more than 15 people, I generally split them and have half my audience discuss the first question and half discuss the second one. Then I'll ask two volunteers to work at flip charts and have a leader from one group discuss the first question: "What kinds of problems do people have because they don't…?" I'll move from group to group and take single responses. The volunteer at one flip chart posts the first response, the second response goes on the second flip chart, and we alternate back and forth. When I've exhausted the responses to the first question, we post them and proceed to the second question: "What happens when you and I do…?"

This simple exercise produces a list of benefits to attain and losses to avoid. Notice that the first question is couched in the third person. It doesn't ask, "What kinds of problems have *you* had because *you* don't…?" Now, everyone in the group may be terrible at delegating or problem solving or whatever, but it's not my purpose, in terms of generating interest, to point out their weaknesses or to have them admit them to one another. By giving me a list of problems they've observed that *other* people have, they also may be admitting their own problems, but they're doing so in a subtle, nonthreatening way.

By the same token, the second question requires positive answers. Of course, the participants may, in fact, be mediocre delegators and problem solvers, but they don't have to admit it. They may be terrible supervisors, but they've seen good supervision, just as they've no doubt seen good delegation and problem solving. We can use the experience of the entire group to draw up a list of very positive reasons why it would be useful to focus on our topic. From their own data, they've spelled out several reasons why it will be valuable to pay attention to the contents of the program.

• *Language*—Make sure you understand the level of linguistic sophistication of your participants. Don't use jargon. Nothing loses an audience faster than language it doesn't understand. *If in doubt, spell it out.* If it's important to use technical terms, define those terms.

Several years ago, I designed a training program that dealt with various financial concepts. In the program was a section that described the importance of having a will. As you perhaps know, a person who dies without a will is considered to have died *intestate.* Many people, however, are not familiar with this word, but they're also unlikely to admit that they don't know its meaning. Consider the likely response if you were to ask participants in a training program, "How many of you do not know what intestate means?" Silence? But how about the more positive, "How many of you know what intestate means?" "Good. Would you define it for us?" Chances are, someone will be able to define the word, so that you, the trainer, can proceed with your presentation.

But, you also face the possibility that no one knows or that someone will guess incorrectly, and you'll have to tell that person he or she is wrong. The best strategy is to define an unfamiliar term immediately after using it. For example, "It's important to understand the consequences of dying intestate, of dying without a will."

The language problem can be more complex when several disciplines are represented by participants in your training program. For example, the chemical terms used to describe an air-pollution problem and the symbols that represent these terms may be part of the scientist's or engineer's everyday vocabulary. If, however, managers from manufacturing are also in attendance, they may have difficulty recalling scientific terms.

In another example, if you're talking economics, the terms may be familiar to an executive, who has acquired this knowledge either through education or on the job. But they may mystify a supervisor or front-line person unless they are explained.

• *Influence*—Who are the decision makers in this group? What are their problems and personal interests? What can you tell them to make their tasks easier? How can you challenge them? How can you build them in as partners in the program? Does your message have the potential of threatening their influence and prestige?

All these questions are important to consider, because we want to build in the expertise of any experts in the program. But one caveat, one warning, here: Do not accept, at face value, someone's personal identification of expertise. Just because someone considers himself or herself an expert doesn't necessarily mean it's so. One consideration, before we run our first program, would be to have the advisory group enlighten us about the experience level of the people in the group. You might also ask those who are sending people to this program for their perceptions of the experience and expertise the individuals in this group will bring.

We also may want to have participants in the group complete an effectiveness grid to assess their expertise. I frequently use an effectiveness grid myself. In one program I conducted, I wanted to gauge the computer literacy of the participants, so I gave each one a computer-literacy grid and asked everyone to rate themselves on their knowledge of computers. This computer-literacy grid, shown on page 115, was designed for managers who were going to participate in a computer-literacy program; its purpose was to familiarize them with computers that were going to be available for their use and that were going to be used extensively in the future by the people who reported to them.

On our grid, we asked them to rate their own computer literacy. If, for example, they felt they knew everything there is to know about computer software, they would rate themselves 100. On the other hand, if they thought that a utility was the gas or electric company that served their homes, they'd probably want to rate themselves 1—because, when we're talking computers, that's not what a utility is.

As people were completing the grid, I went around the room to see how they were scoring themselves. If somebody was scoring himself or herself extremely high, it *might* have meant—and let me emphasize *might* —that this person had a lot of computer experience and/or expertise. To find out just how skilled in computers a high scorer really was, I would kneel down next to him or her and, without making it obvious to everybody in the room, say something like, "It seems you've had a lot of experience in this area and I'd like to be able to tap into that. I wonder if you would be willing to do some of the demonstrations that are part of this program in front of the group. Also, when we break into work groups, would you consider not being in a group but working with me instead to check on the other groups?"

Now, one of two things is going to be true here. If the person really is an expert, I'm likely to get a response like, "Sure, no problem. I'd be happy to help." If he or she isn't an expert, however, I'll hear something like, "Well, I really came here just to be a participant." Either way, I've gotten some worthwhile information. First, if the person is an expert, I've helped build his or her experience into the program. In the case of those who just think they're experts, I've taken some steps that will help minimize disruption and the exchange of misinformation; if they really want to be involved and verbalize what they know, they'll carefully consider the possibility of being asked to "perform" before the entire group.

Occasionally, I will encounter somebody with an ego that just won't quit. Even though this person has very little or no experience at all, he or she will say "Sure, no problem" to my request for assistance. But just because I've asked somebody to come up and do a demonstration or be prepared to help work with groups rather than be part of them doesn't mean I'm going to encourage an obviously inexperienced person to do that. I don't want to put people in situations where they're going to fail.

To those people who have volunteered to share their expertise, I say, "There will be times, I'm sure, when questions will come up, and I'd like you to help answer them. So when someone in the group asks a question that seems relevant to your expertise, I'll look over at you. If you nod, I'll know that it's a question you can handle."

Never yet has an inexperienced person made eye contact with me when a question was being asked by someone in the group. That tells me that, if these individuals aren't willing or able to respond to questions the group might ask, then I certainly don't want them to come up in front of the group and be embarrassed.

• *Situational Elements*—What is the size of the group? How many people you have will dictate the amount of equipment you need, the amount of space you need, and so on.

Location? What kinds of facilities do you have for the training program?

Are they ideal or less than ideal? Are the chairs comfortable or uncomfortable? Are you able to rearrange the room from time to time just for variety?

What time of day is the program going to be offered? Generally speaking, people are fresher in the morning, if that's their normal time to start work, than they are in the afternoon. If your program is scheduled for the afternoon, you'll need more involvement and participation to keep people focused and alert. All these should be considered before we even begin to design the program.

Step 3. Decide Your Aim

To determine you aims, or goals, ask yourself: "As a result of this training, what do I want people to know, feel, and do?" Psychologists have identified three domains of learning. The *cognitive* domain deals with knowledge. The *affective* domain deals with feelings and emotions. And the *psychomotor* domain deals with skills. As trainers, your aim will be to affect one or more of these *know, feel, do* areas.

You can narrow your focus by asking yourself these questions. What do I want participants to know that they didn't know before? How do I want them to feel? Do I want them to have a more positive attitude toward the subject, to be excited about implementing the subject, to feel self-confident about their ability to perform? What do I want them to be able to do that they haven't done before? How are the results of this training going to be measured and evaluated? Do people have to perform at a particular skill level? How are the payers and senders going to measure success?

INSIDER'S TIP

One technique that I will use is creating a group mind-map. This is a process that is outlined in Chapter Nine. We put up three or four sheets of flip chart paper with the central topic in the center and the people who know the topic well—my "Subject-Matter Experts"—will begin creating a mind-map of all the content that we're thinking of covering in a particular training program or all of the things that people need to know about a specific subject.

As that mind-map is developed, it gives us a visual representation of the subject and, because it's more visual than a traditional outline, it allows us to see gaps—what's not there. When we look at a traditional outline, we have a tendency to evaluate what's there. It's much more difficult to see what's missing. The mind-map allows us to see the holes that there might be in the content. It also allows us to sequence the material by looking at the material as a whole and then looking at the various orders in which we might sequence the material.

To answer these tough questions, you must thoroughly research your topic. Collect more information than you plan to use. Overprepare and then boil it down. How many times have you seen presenters run out of content because their audience was better informed than they had anticipated? Or hit bottom before getting to the level of depth that their participants needed?

How much do you already know about your topic, and how much does your audience need to know? You'll have a research gap to fill if your audience needs to know more than you already know. Which of your ideas needs more support than you've provided, and where can you find that support efficiently? Don't scrape the bottom of the barrel. There's nothing worse than having an hour left and nothing to say. It's better to leave participants feeling that more could be said. In other words, it's better to run out of time before you run out of material.

Here are some quick research tips:

1. What articles on the topic have appeared in trade or industry publications in the past 12-24 months?

2. What articles have appeared in business or popular publications in the past 12-24 months?

3. What books have been published on the subject in the past year?

4. What topics appear again and again on industry conference programs?

Using these tips can help you become more aware of the trends and the needs that may exist in your industry or organization.

Step 4. Plan Your Approach

How are you going to get favorable attention? We've already touched on one way—asking questions, such as "What kinds of problems have you observed?" To introduce the program, consider answering these questions that the participants may ask: "What's in it for me? How will I be able to do my job faster, better, easier? What benefits can I gain? What losses can I avoid?"

It's important to be aware of the difference between an opening for a program and an icebreaker. People are going to remember what we do first, best. It's important, therefore, that what we do really fits the program. One mistake trainers tend to make is to mistake an icebreaker for an opening. An icebreaker may get people acquainted, but it may not be relevant to the program content. Here are my tests for an effective opener:

1. Does it break preoccupation? People may be physically present in a room, but not mentally present. They could be preoccupied by other things—work left undone at the job, an argument they had at home that morning, a frustrating traffic delay on the way to the seminar, or maybe just wondering whether or not this content is going to be useful—at least

useful enough to justify being away from the job. We need to break through that preoccupation and get people focused on the class and not on external concerns.

2. Does it facilitate networking? Does my opening help people become comfortable with one another? When tension goes up, retention goes down. People may be sitting there concerned about whether or not they fit in, whether they know as much as other people in the room, whether or not they're really going to be able to contribute. The longer a class, the more important it is to help people get comfortable with one another.

3. Is it relevant to the program? Can people see the logical tie-in between the opening that I'm doing and the content of the course?

4. Does it maintain or enhance self-esteem? I believe that one of the purposes of training is for people to leave impressed with themselves, not intimidated by the instructor—excited about what they now know that they didn't know before, excited about what they can now do that they couldn't do before and with greater confidence in themselves than before. We can begin that process of confidence and excellence right in the opening of our program by making people feel good about themselves and the fact that they're there.

5. Is it fun for both the trainer and the participants? The fun factor may not always be important, but having some fun at the beginning of the program can help people realize that this is not going to be another boring lecture-educational experience, but in fact they're going to learn things and at the same time be able to have some fun.

6. Is their curiosity aroused? Curiosity can be a very powerful motivator. In the Appendix, you'll find four tested openers that we've been able to use in a variety of training programs: Four Facts, the Penny Exercise, the Alphabet Search, and Uniquenesess and Commonalities. You'll see that while each of these is distinctively different, each of them meets the tests of effective openers that we've given here.

Finally, decide what transition you're going to use as you proceed from the introduction to the main content. Here's a good place to identify and clarify the group's goals. One way almost all trainers could significantly improve the effect of their training would be to strengthen the beginning and end of their presentation. From the participants perspective, the beginning must gain their interest and create a sense of anticipation for what lies ahead.

Step 5. *Plan Your Lesson Development*

Whenever I design a training program, I make a brief outline, because I don't want to be tied to my notes. Sometimes, trainers are so tied to their format that, if they can't follow it exactly as planned, they can't deliver the content. How many times have you heard a presenter say, "I lost my transparencies. There's not going to be a class." Or, "The VCR doesn't work, so I can't play the tape I brought. There's not going to be a class."

In college, I learned this little rhyme:

The room was hushed, the speaker mute.
He'd left his notes in his other suit.

If we're masters of our content before we begin to deliver, we won't suffer this humiliating fate.

Within my base outline, I first must consider my manner of presentation. The longer the presentation, the more variety and changes of pace I need.

Tony Buzan in his book, *Use Both Sides of Your Brain,* says that his research indicates that the average adult can listen with *understanding* for ninety minutes, but can only listen with *retention* for twenty minutes. That means that we need a distinct change-up or change of pace every twenty minutes. Based on Buzan's information, we at Creative Training Techniques have evolved the 90/20/8 rule: no module we teach ever runs more than ninety minutes, the pace is changed at least every twenty minutes, and we try to find a way to involve people in the content every eight minutes.

Second, I consider learner participation and response. Remember, my goal is to tap people's experiences and to have the program be instructor-led but participant-centered. How will I get and keep participants involved? The methods of instruction in Chapter Five will give you ideas that you can apply to get your participants more involved.

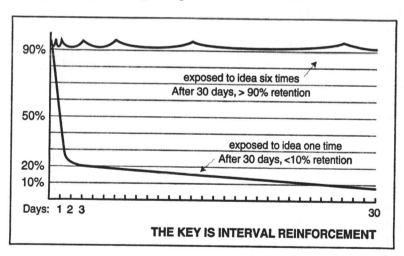

Third, I decide how I will review previous content, which I'll need to reinforce constantly. Albert Mehrabian presents some fascinating information in his book *Silent Messages.* In his research, he found that if people were exposed to an idea one time, at the end of 30 days they retained less than 10 percent. But if they were exposed to an idea six times, with interval reinforcement, at the end of 30 days they retained more than 90 percent. Interval reinforcement means that the idea was presented once and then reviewed perhaps ten minutes later, an hour later, a day later, three days later, a week later, two weeks later, three weeks later. In other words, there were intervals between each review.

Finally, I determine how to vary my transitions from point to point. The importance of this step lies in "Pike's First Law of Adult Learning": Adults are babies with big bodies. Think for a moment about the kinds of activities children pursue in preschool and kindergarten. They paint, play with blocks, color, play games, tell and listen to stores—all kinds of hands-on involvement carried out in a room conducive to participation. As they advance to first, second, and third grades, children tend to be lined up in rows and talked *at*. And the more they grow and mature, the less they involve themselves actively in the learning process. The older they get and the more experiences they acquire, the less they get to use them.

Hence, my conclusion that adults are babies with big bodies. Just as young children can learn well through direct experience, so can adults, particularly when they're allowed to use their shared life experiences. Remember what Confucius said? "What I hear, I forget; what I see, I remember; but what I do, I understand." If there is a way to get involvement, I want to use it, because the focus of training is to help people get results, not simply to cover content. I haven't done my job if I've only covered content. What counts is the application that participants can make once the program is over.

Step 6. Plan Your Lesson Application

Remember that all of our participants are tuned to two radio stations, one we've already given: *WII-FM: What's In It For Me?* How will this help me do my job faster, better, easier? What are the benefits that I'll gain? What are the losses I'll avoid?"

The second radio station they're tuned to is *MMFI-AM: Make Me Feel Important About Myself.* I believe that one of the purposes of training is for participants to leave impressed with themselves, not intimidated with the instructor—excited about what they now know, excited about what they can now do, and with greater feelings of confidence in both what they've learned and what they can now accomplish.

The application step is the step that helps reinforce both what's in it for them and their own personal feelings of accomplishment. Helping them apply what they've learned is an important key to helping participants both know and feel that they've really accomplished something.

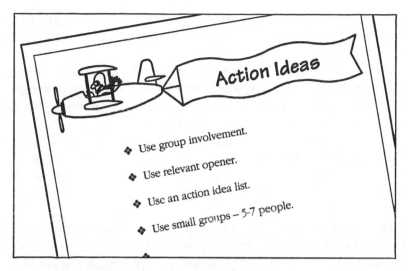

Action Ideas

❖ Use group involvement.

❖ Use relevant opener.

❖ Use an action idea list.

❖ Use small groups – 5-7 people.

People are looking for practical and personal solutions, for answers to the question "How do *I* use this?" To help them find the answers, I use what I call an action idea list in many of my programs. I repeatedly ask people to keep track of useful ideas that they can apply back on the job. From time to time, the group reviews the list, sharing key action ideas and adding to each other's lists. This is a natural way to build in lesson application.

Remember, people don't argue with their own data. If I say something, I'm not objective because I'm teaching the material. But if they say it, their own experience validates it.

Step 7. Plan a Carry-over Activity

If you're doing multiple sessions, plan an activity that will encourage participants to decide how they can use what they've learned. How will they report back their progress and problems? Ask them to take three minutes to answer these questions: What's the most important thing I've learned? And what am I going to do about it?

Step 8. Gather the Materials and Prepare the Room

I'm sure you remember Murphy's Law: Whatever can go wrong, will. But are you familiar with O'Toole's Corollary, which states that Murphy was an optimist?

Here you are, ready to launch a two-week training program, and you want to make positive initial contact with your group. You want to get participants excited and involved by creating a sense of anticipation. You turn the switch on the overhead projector to project a visual. But the light bulb is burned out, and there's no spare. You go over to the flip chart and turn to a clean sheet, only to find that there's no more paper. Or there's plenty of paper, but the first two or three markers you try to use have dried out. (By the way, that's another corollary to Murphy's Law: All markers run dry at the same time!)

You haven't even opened your mouth yet, but you can sense the kind of anticipation your participants now feel about the next two weeks—and it has nothing to do with your content. So, gather your materials and prepare the room *before* you launch your program.

My goal is always to be set up and ready to go 15 minutes before any participants arrive. There are two good reasons for this time limit.

First, I can take care of any glitch before participants arrive. If handouts don't show up or visual equipment breaks down, I can arrange alternative delivery methods.

The second, and perhaps more important, reason is that I like to interact with participants for 15 minutes before a class begins. This demonstrates my belief that the participants are as important as the content.

Getting acquainted with participants helps them feel comfortable with you and vice versa. It also provides you, the trainer, with further insights into the group and helps you gauge their readiness to learn, their interest, their reasons for attending, and their level of experience. It lets you address questions and concerns they may have. And it helps you relax and move naturally into the program itself.

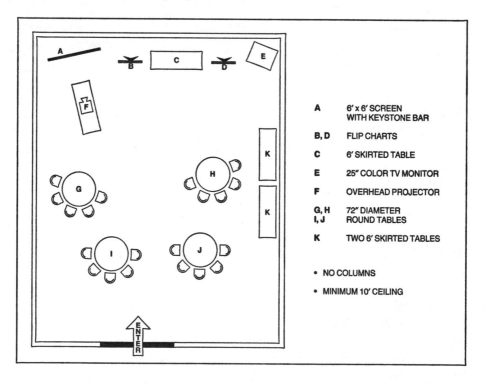

A	6′ x 6′ SCREEN WITH KEYSTONE BAR
B, D	FLIP CHARTS
C	6′ SKIRTED TABLE
E	25″ COLOR TV MONITOR
F	OVERHEAD PROJECTOR
G, H	72″ DIAMETER
I, J	ROUND TABLES
K	TWO 6′ SKIRTED TABLES

• NO COLUMNS

• MINIMUM 10′ CEILING

How We Set Our Rooms

The physical environment that you do your presentation in can have a great deal of impact on your program. Here are just a few of the things to take note of on the room diagram on the previous page that we use for our Creative Training Techniques seminars. First, notice that the screen is set at a diagonal for the overhead projector in the corner of the room to maximize everybody being able to see it. The bottom of the screen is placed approximately 42″ above the floor level and we always get a minimum of a 10′ ceiling height in order to make sure that we can project the visuals high enough for everybody to see.

Notice that the participants are seated at half rounds which immediately makes them feel part of a group. Also, we try to minimize the rounds to five to seven people. We always put a few less chairs than we think we're going to need. We stack extra chairs. It's always better to be adding chairs once the tables are filled the way you want them to than to have more chairs than you need and to have some tables with too few participants. We also allow plenty of table space for putting materials that people are either going to pick up themselves or that you are going to be distributing later. People enter from the rear of the room so that any latecomers are not a distraction in the way that they would be if they were entering from either the side of the room or the front of the room.

The color monitor that we use for displaying computer graphics is on a standard 60″ stand to have the visuals high enough for participants to see them clearly. For flipcharts, we use graphed paper that have light blue 1″ squares on them. It makes it easier to create lines, charts, and also to print on an even line across the pad.

POWER TIPS ON PREPARATION

Prepare Your Talks But Don't Memorize Word for Word

Practice your talk once or twice, preferably aloud, before you give it to the group. You can do this privately or before family or friends. But don't overdo the practicing. Just try to fix the sequence of points in your mind. Too much rehearsing leads to slavish memorizing, which will make your talk sound mechanical. Memorized presentations often lack spontaneity and naturalness, because the speaker concentrates on recalling words instead of ideas.

Memorizing also makes it difficult to refer easily to any "new" material, such as something said by a previous speaker or by the person who introduced you. If you are distracted by what goes on around you (such as a loud sneeze in the audience, a door slamming, a waiter dropping a tray, etc.), there is a good chance you will falter and forget what comes next if you're a slave to memory.

Express Your Ideas Clearly and Concisely

Concentrate on communicating worthwhile ideas in order to help others, not to make an outstanding personal impression. Polished words and fancy phrases are no substitute for a good idea sincerely and simply expressed. As Aristotle said, "Think as the wise men do, but speak as the common people do."

Build the Outline

In preparing any talk, first LIMIT your topic to one specific idea. Second, SELECT specific material suited to that limited purpose. Third, ARRANGE your material, your illustrations, examples, facts, and statistics in a coherent order.

A skeleton outline based on such abstract words as "introduction," "body," and "conclusion" won't help you much. Instead, use phrases like "take hold," "transmit," and "drive home." Start with a word picture or a story that is relevant to your dominant purpose that "takes hold" of your listeners' attention. After "transmitting" your idea and the specific incidents, illustrations, or other evidence to back it up, you're ready to "drive home" your point with an effective conclusion. This might be a brief summary of your idea, a quotation, a call for action, or even a poem. It should highlight your talk and nail your point with intensity.

Use the KFD Principles to Identify Learner Response

We covered the know-feel-do principle in the Eight Steps to Proper Preparation. Now let's explore these three domains more thoroughly. First, we must ask ourselves, "What new information or content do the participants need to *know*?" This addresses the cognitive aspect of your training presentation.

Secondly, we should ask, "How do we want them to *feel*?" Do we want them to feel motivated, inspired, energetic, sad, angry? How do we want them to react to the presentation? Do we want them to feel challenged to use these new insights? Do we want them to feel dissatisfied with present behaviors, present procedures? Do we want them to feel confident that they can use their new skills or knowledge?

Finally, what do we want people to *do*? What actions do we want them to take? Since learning doesn't take place until behavior has changed, we want participants to convert ideas into action.

Use Information Overload to Insure You Are Prepared

The third step to effective preparation suggests that you'll want to gather more information than you'll be able to use. It is much easier to boil down too much information than it is to expand or puff up minimal information. This preparation step will depend upon your group members, their experience level, and their backgrounds. Much of the information you gather may be simplistic or fundamental to some groups but new and necessary to others. To find out what information your attendees need to know as well as what topics are of concern to them, consider doing a content analysis.

1. Collect the last 12 months of several publications devoted to the concerns of your target group, the group for whom you're preparing a presentation or training program.

2. Starting with the most current issues, list the relevant topics covered and the amount of print or space devoted to each. Then compare this with the amount of coverage these topics received 12 months ago.

Exclude feature articles from this initial analysis. You may want to share information from feature articles with trainees, but don't use them to analyze whether or not specific topics may enhance your program.

3. Once you've completed the current month's issues and compared them with those of 12 months ago, analyze the remaining issues of your publications (magazines and/or newspapers). As you list your topics, also list the amount of space devoted to each. You may find that something that had merited only a few inches of space four months ago has 12 or 18 inches devoted to it today. You also may notice that a "hot" topic 10 or 11 months ago is getting much less coverage now.

Issues that receive the most recent attention probably will provide the greatest stimulus for attendees at your presentation. This *quantitative* part of your content analysis will give you broad topics.

4. To do a *qualitative* analysis, read the material about the most relevant topics and pinpoint those that are most helpful. Be consistent in your review. You can't simply use one or two publications or use only two or three months' worth of publications. Review as many as you can over a period of 12 months.

Another way you can gather information is to create a system of files on training topics that you're going to present. For example, if you are developing a program or a presentation on Creative Training Techniques, start a Creative Training Techniques file; clip out pertinent articles you come across and put them in that file. When you're ready to design the program, you can review that file.

Note the titles of books and page references you'll want to refer to on three by five cards and insert them into the file, too.

USE THE AIDA FORMULA IN
DEVELOPING YOUR PRESENTATION

AIDA is an acronym based on the names of the four major steps into which a presentation or segment of a training program can be divided. (Music lovers will also recognize it as the name of a famous opera by Verdi.)

Attention

At the beginning of any presentation, you must get the attention of the group. One of the most obvious ways is to ask a question. Members of your audience may be preoccupied with their own conversations; when you solicit an answer to a question, you break through that preoccupation and gain their attention.

If, for example, you were running a program on decision making, you might ask a group of managers, "What kinds of problems do some managers have because they don't make decisions effectively?" Or, to begin a program on budgeting, you might ask, "What kinds of problems do people encounter when they don't handle money well?" As your participants begin responding, the side conversations will stop. You can then record participant responses on a flip chart.

There are three advantages to this particular technique.

1. You break through preoccupation and gain favorable attention.

2. You immediately involve your audience.

3. The question you ask begins to build a case for why your topic, or this particular part of the training program, is important. As people give their answers, they're acknowledging that a particular problem exists, and, as the list grows longer, some people in your group can identify with aspects of that problem. You're not only gaining attention; you're also demonstrating why the particular topic you're presenting is relevant.

Interest

Here's where you begin to answer the question "What's in it for me?" Every person to whom we will ever make a presentation is tuned to radio station *WII-FM: What's In It For Me?* As we gather the information we want to present and as we recognize that there are things we want our audience to know, feel, and do as a result of our presentation, we also have to determine how each participant will benefit from knowing what we want them to know, feeling what we want them to feel, doing what we want them to do.

Desire

In the desire step, we begin to share the content, the practical how-to's, that we suggested were forthcoming in the attention and interest steps.

Here's where we offer the means toward the end results. How can I solve the problem, close more sales, make more effective decisions, appraise performance more effectively, train more creatively? These questions are explored in the desire step.

Action

This wrap-up step is based on your asking the group, "What actions are you going to take? What did you learn, and how are you going to put your learning into practice?" Ideally, their feedback will indicate to you that training has provided a new, more effective way to do something and that they're willing to give it a try.

✔ **CHECK YOURSELF**

List the techniques you use on a regular basis. Do you rely on them and exclude others? Try one new method in your next presentation just to add spice and variety.

BRIGHT IDEA

DETERMINING THE MANNER AND METHOD OF PRESENTATION: INVOLVEMENT TECHNIQUES AND CONTENT APPLICATION

In making presentations, we can use a wide variety of techniques. As you prepare your program, consider the following possibilities, most of which eventually will be described in greater detail. Here, we simply want to give a sampling of the kinds of methods and involvement techniques available to you. (See list in Chapter Five.)

There are at least two or three effective ways to make any point we want to convey. Take a look at your own methods of presenting. List the techniques you use on a fairly regular basis. Do you find yourself relying upon the same ones to the exclusion of many others? If this is the case, you might want to consider adopting other presentation techniques and methods to put variety, creativity, spontaneity, and impact into your training.

APPLICATION OR CARRY-OVER ACTIVITIES

The final part of our preparation is to spend some time thinking how we're going to help people put into practice the things they've learned. One way is to introduce activities that help people decide how they will apply their new knowledge. One of the simplest such activities is to ask the participants, "What have you learned? How are you going to put it into practice?"

LEARNER MOTIVATION

3

Making Sure the Audience Keeps Learning
After You've Finished Teaching

"Have you ever faced a group of less-than-eager participants, people who didn't necessarily want to be there?" In every audience of trainers I've presented to, more than 90 percent of the hands go up when I ask that question. My response is: "That means you've been in training longer than a week!"

Most of our classes and meetings, whether one-on-one or small groups, are attended by people who don't want to be there. Sometimes it's because of pressures on the job, and sometimes they can't see the relationship between themselves and the content being covered. So how can we motivate these people?

BASIC PRINCIPLES OF MOTIVATION

Learning tends to be effective to the extent that the student is properly motivated. And what is motivation? Basically, it's what incites a person to action. Motive/action: Motivation is a motive for acting, a reason for doing what we do. And almost all of us can justify or explain our actions.

Three Basic Principles of Motivation

1. You cannot motivate other people.
2. All people are motivated.

You might say, "Hey, wait! I know some people who are late two mornings a week and sick the other three days. You mean to tell me they're motivated?" My response would be, "Absolutely! They're more motivated to be sick and late and absent than they are to be on time and effective."

Almost all of us have reasons, which are valid for us, for why we do what we do. So all people are motivated. Maybe not the way you and I think they ought to be, but they are motivated.

3. People do things for their reasons, not your reasons.

This gets back to the fact that people are tuned to the radio station *WII-FM: What's In It For Me?* People have *their* reasons for doing things. Principle Number One states that you cannot motivate other people. True enough—but you *can* create a climate or an environment in which a person is self-motivated.

This underscores what we talked about in the previous chapter, about getting people's attention and answering for them: "What's in it for me? How will I benefit if I learn this information, if I feel these feelings, if I take the action that's suggested here?"

The question I must have uppermost in my mind as I approach a training program is: What's the payoff—for the participant, for the participant's boss, and for the person who's paying for the training? It's important that not only you and I clearly see the benefits of training but that these individuals do as well.

Over and over again, as I've observed trainers, I see the basic principles of motivation violated. It's almost as if they wanted to kill the motivation in their adult learners. Over time, I've identified five key ways to squelch motivation.

FIVE WAYS TO SQUELCH MOTIVATION

1. Have Little Personal Contact

Be the last one there, the first one to leave, and make it clear that lunch and coffee breaks belong to you. You may have to teach content, but you certainly don't have to relate to anyone.

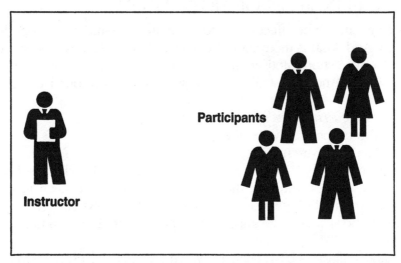

Several years ago, when I was living in Colorado, I was leading a series of human-relations and communications seminars that were given in ten three-hour sessions. Not only was I conducting the courses, I also was responsible for marketing them. It wasn't too long before I was leading three-hour seminars on Monday, Tuesday, and Thursday nights, on Wednesday and Friday mornings, and one weekend a month.

Needless to say, this plus the marketing gave me a rather full schedule. So I thought it would really be helpful if someone else could lead some of these seminars. After completing one particular course, a participant, who had an MBA and who was executive director of a very large volunteer organization in Denver, came up to me and said, "If you're interested in having someone in our group be a seminar leader, I'd sure like to learn how to do it."

I was excited about this opportunity. So I asked my mother, who was my receptionist at the time, if she could help out on Tuesday nights— opening the seminar room, greeting people as they came in, putting on the coffee, and so on. Then Tim, the new leader, would come and conduct the sessions.

The sessions ran from 7 to 10 o'clock. My mother would be there around 6:30, put the coffee on, get the name tags out, and greet people as they came in. At 6:59 on the button, Tim would show up. He would run the seminar exactly the way it was supposed to be run. Then, at 10:01, he was the first one out the door. My mom, however, would stay around while people talked—sometimes to her, sometimes to one another—and finally she would lock up the training facility around 10:30 and go home.

Tim wasn't able to lead the seventh session, so I came in to run the class. By the time the coffee break was over, 75 percent of the students had asked me why my mother wasn't teaching the course! Now, my mother hadn't gone to college, and she had no experience in the subjects under discussion, but she had made a more positive impression on the group's participants than Tim had. Why? Because she had demonstrated that she cared about them personally.

If you want to squelch motivation, show up just in time to make your presentation, leave immediately after, and make sure you stay unavailable during breaks.

2. Get Participants in a Passive Mood and Keep Them There
This means, for example, that you don't allow any questions. When the participants come back from lunch, start out by showing a film. Raise the room temperature five to ten degrees, and make sure you don't have any water available. Speak in a monotone. Avoid eye contact. All these things will put people in a passive mood and keep them there.

3. Assume the Class Will Apply What It Is Taught
Don't bother with specific examples. Remember, these people are adults, so you don't have to draw pictures for them. Just give them straight content. You can cover more in less time if you don't bother with illustrations. After all, it's your responsibility simply to present. It's their responsibility as adults to apply what you present.

4. Be Quick to Criticize

Remember the management adage that "criticism should be delivered in public; praise, if any, given in private."

If somebody asks a dumb question, say so. If somebody misses something, point it out with a tactful comment such as, "You know, you just asked a question that I answered not more than three minutes ago. Perhaps one of the other participants was more alert than you."

5. Make Participants Feel Stupid for Asking Questions in Class

A couple of years ago, I attended a presentation made by a guest speaker to about 40 training professionals. What I witnessed illustrates a number of points I've been making and will continue to make throughout this manual.

The speaker began by saying, "I don't really know why I'm here because I don't do any training. However, the people who invited me seem to think I've got something to say, so I guess I'll go ahead and say it. I could have been better prepared, but I thought this presentation was next week. I didn't know until I got a phone call reminding me yesterday that it was actually today."

With that, he picked up a piece of chalk, which was supposed to fool us into thinking he might actually use a visual aid. After about 45 minutes, he asked, "Do you believe that if you change attitudes, you will change behavior, or that if you change behavior, you will change attitudes?"

He paused and looked at the group for a response. No one said anything for about 20 or 30 seconds. So I raised my hand, and he asked, "Do you want to give it a try?"

I said, "I believe that if you change attitudes, you will change behavior, but that if you change behavior, you will sometimes change attitudes."

He replied, "Do you still believe that? All the literature indicates…" and he went on in that fashion.

My immediate thought was, "All *what* literature?" I considered myself fairly well-read on the subject, and I thought there were points to be made on both sides of the issue.

He continued his presentation. "One time," he said, "we did some research for an insurance company that was bothered by a particular problem. When they hired a new life insurance agent, that agent's sales performance would increase for about 18 months, but then it would drop and level off. The client wanted to find out what happened at 18 months, almost consistently across all agents, that caused that drop in sales performance.

"We evaluated all kinds of things, considered all kinds of options, examined all the possibilities. Yet we found only one significant thing happening at 18 months."

The speaker asked the audience, "And what do you think that was?" He waited for a response.

Finally, I raised my hand, and he acknowledged me by saying, "You want to try again?" I said, "They ran out of relatives?"

He glared at me and snapped, "That's wrong. Anybody else want to try?" Nobody did.

I didn't attempt to answer any other questions during his presentation. And, as a matter of fact, no one else would answer any either.

At the end of his presentation, the speaker got a polite round of applause. He went up to the president of the group and gloated, "I really had some doubts about doing this presentation, but it was obviously well-received. I'd like to come back." And, on that note, he left.

About 35 of the 40 people went to a nearby lounge, where the real learning took place. "Did you hear when he said that?" "Did you see when he did that?" Only then did the participants dare ask questions and involve themselves in the experience.

Think back to the five ways to squelch motivation, and you'll see how effectively the speaker in my example employed them all.

1. Have little personal contact: he was the last one there and the first to leave.

2. Get people in a passive mood and keep them there: he asked two questions in nearly two hours, not exactly what you'd call involvement.

3. Assume they'll apply the information, so skip the examples: he did have one good illustration—about the insurance agents, which I'll return to—but it was the only one in a lengthy presentation.

4. Be quick to criticize: he was great at that.

5. Make participants feel stupid for asking questions: he not only made us feel stupid for asking questions, he made us feel stupid for trying to answer them.

True, this unskilled presenter did use specific examples, yet he was certainly critical. For example, when he asked the question, "What do you think caused performance to drop?," he squelched my answer about running out of relatives. He might have said something like, "You know that's an interesting answer. It was certainly considered as a possibility. But it just didn't turn out that way. Does someone else have a guess?" That more tactful approach would have encouraged further responses.

He did use one good illustration, though, and I'd like to discuss it further. When his organization did research for the insurance company, it found that, for the first 18 months, the new agent would go to a prospective customer's home and ask questions like: "How long have you lived here? What is your mortgage? What are the payments? How many children do you have? What are your educational plans for your children?" After about 45 minutes of asking questions, the agent would say, "By using your answers to my questions, I can formulate certain plans and strategies that can help you achieve your financial goals."

After asking the same questions over and over again for 18 months, each agent became an expert. He or she could look at a customer's home and conclude, "They've lived here 4.6 years, the mortgage is $86,900, and the payments are $869.50. They have 2.6 kids, and 1.6 are going to go to college." In ten minutes, the agent could tell the customer what he or she needed. And once the agents stopped asking and started telling, their sales results dropped.

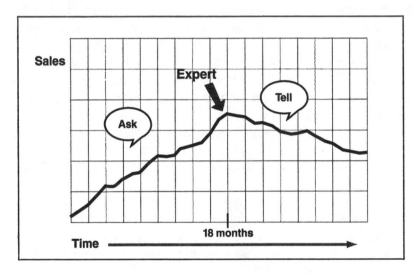

How many times do we as trainers tell our participants things that they could have discovered for themselves—if only we had asked? Remember, people don't argue with their own data. If they think something is true, then for them it is true. But if *you* say it's true, it may be suspect. After all, you've got to believe it; you're the instructor!

Furthermore, nobody likes experts. We want to knock them off their pedestals. Let's say, for example, that your ten-year-old daughter comes running home from school one day and says, "Look, Mom! Look, Dad! Can you solve this equation for 'X'?" You stare blankly at the problem and finally confess, "No, I can't." When she says, in a superior tone, "Well, I can!" your response might be something like, "Great. But is your room clean? Have you taken the garbage out yet? What about the book report that was due last week?" Why does your child's know-it-all attitude annoy you? Because no one likes it when someone—even your child, of whom you're very proud—says, in effect, "I know something you don't. But if you're lucky, I may share the information with you, stupid!"

Yet imagine that the same daughter came running in and said, "Look, Mom! Look, Dad! Look what I learned to do today. I can solve this equation by multiplying the top by 4 to get 36, and then I multiply the bottom by 3. Next, I subtract…"

Our likely response to *this* child's enthusiasm and desire to share new learning is: "Chip off the old block! Have some cookies and some milk. Honey, come here and look at this! Let's save this for Gramma!"

The basic difference between these two scenarios is simply this: "Let me share with you what I've been learning" instead of "I know something you don't."

Just as we can kill motivation in our participants, we can also create an environment where they motivate themselves. Over time, I've identified eleven ways we can create that environment.

HOW TO MOTIVATE ADULTS

1. Create a Need

Remember, that people are constantly asking themselves: "What's in it for me?"

Since they're all tuned to that radio station *WII-FM*, make sure you spend some time at the beginning of every presentation talking about what's in it for them.

- Why do they need this information?
- How will they benefit from it?
- How can they make use of it in a practical, real way?

2. Develop a Sense of Personal Responsibility

Remember the basic principle of motivation: You cannot motivate other people; you can only create a climate or an environment in which they can motivate themselves. Each individual is responsible for the learning, but it is your responsibility to create the best possible climate in which that learning can take place.

An effective way to do this is to give participants an opportunity at the beginning of the class to indicate:

- What expectations they have,
- What outcomes they expect, and
- What they're willing to do to achieve those results.

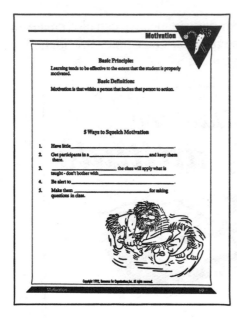

You can also distribute partial handouts that participants must complete themselves in order for the material to be useful. You can make the group responsible for various learning activities. And you can make participants responsible for the simple mechanics of the class, such as returning from breaks on time.

3. Create and Maintain Interest

One effective way to do this is to encourage question asking throughout. Questions generate interest; questions create alertness. There is only one thing we are more conditioned to answer than a question—and that's the telephone!

Another way you can create and maintain interest is to use variety. You don't need to rely exclusively upon games or role plays. You can use the various techniques and methods discussed in Chapter Four. For example, you can use charts, discussion, lectures, films, overhead transparencies, projects, and case studies. Mix and match a variety of techniques in order to grab your participants' attention and engage them in the learning experience.

Another involvement technique is to give people handouts for them to complete. Two examples are partial transparencies on which they fill in key words and partial outlines that they complete as the session proceeds. This activity keeps participants involved in the learning process and also gives them something of value that they can refer to in the future.

This simple device also allows you to cover more material in less time. A well-prepared handout indicates in a nonverbal way that you're thoroughly and thoughtfully prepared for the presentation. It tells your participants that you cared enough about this presentation to prepare superior supplemental materials.

4. Structure Experiences to Apply Content to Life

In most of the presentations you make and the training you do, people want to know: "How will this work for me?" and "Will this really help me make better decisions, solve more problems, make more sales, etc.?"

They want *practical* applications. Sure, theory is important, but people must see how that theory can be put into practice so that their jobs can be done faster, easier, better and their lives and work can be more interesting.

5. Give Recognition, Encouragement, and Approval

William James, the Harvard psychologist, said that the greatest need of every human being is the need for appreciation. Most of us are like dry sponges waiting for a drop of appreciation. People are very quick to point out when we've done something wrong; they're slow to acknowledge that we've done something right. When we finally do something that is so absolutely right we can hardly believe we've done it, we wait for somebody to acknowledge our accomplishment. And we wait and wait and wait. Finally, we grab someone and explain in full color and vivid detail this absolutely right thing we've done. And we're likely to hear something like, "Well, it's about time" or "Isn't that your job?" or "Isn't that what you're paid for?"

We, as trainers, must recognize that need for appreciation in the classroom. One good way to do this is by repeating comments that people may make. For example, someone might approach you during a break and comment about something that was said during the session. As you begin the next segment of your presentation, you could use this brief exchange in a positive way: "Fran made an interesting comment during the break, one that certainly applies to the things we've been exploring in this program. I think it bears repeating."

What's been accomplished by employing this simple technique?

- You gave recognition.
- You not only encouraged Fran but you encouraged the rest of the group to become more involved.
- You certainly demonstrated by your approval that you want feedback and comments.

6. Foster Wholesome Competition

Wholesome competition enables people to measure themselves with themselves. It lets them say, "I don't compete with you; I compete with myself." And ask, "Where am I right now, and how can I improve myself?"

7. Get Excited Yourself

You certainly can't expect people to get more excited about your program or content or presentation than you are. So let people see your own genuine enthusiasm for your topic.

There are two ways to do this, no matter what your personal style. One, be available. Being available to participants at least fifteen minutes before the class starts shows our interest, enthusiasm, and excitement for the subject and for the participants themselves.

Secondly, give eye contact. People that are not confident in their subject or are disinterested in it have a tendency to never look at their participants. They have mastered what I call the "Soft Glaze." They either focus about twelve inches above everybody's head or are constantly looking at their notes. But the one thing they don't do is give eye contact.

8. Establish Long-range Objectives

Help people realize how they can benefit—in the long run—as they increase their level of confidence in the areas you're discussing, presenting, and training them. Here is where adults differ from children. You can give a child a task, and the child simply goes to work and does it. The task doesn't necessarily need to relate to anything. But adults like to see the big picture; then they can concentrate on the individual pieces.

9. See the Value of Internal Motives

While you, as a trainer, may have organizational objectives, individual, or internal, desires and objectives may be far more motivational to program participants. Recognize and encourage these more personal motives.

10. Intensify Interpersonal Relationships

Give people in the class the opportunity to meet and socialize with one another, and also make yourself available to them. That means being there early, staying late, and making yourself available during the breaks, lunches, and social times.

Connecting with your participants on a one-on-one basis can be extremely valuable, but helping them connect with one another on a one-on-one basis can be even more valuable.

After the training is over, it may be very difficult for you to stay in touch and be available. After all, tomorrow or next week you'll be working with a different group and it will be difficult to be available to this group. But if we connect them with one another so that they are comfortable enough in calling one another after the class, then we've expanded their network, their relationships and the support that they have available to make sure that they can implement the content of your training program.

11. Give Them a Choice

For example, develop two or three case studies, and give participants a choice of which one to examine in depth. Or design three carry-over activities and ask them to do one of the three.

All of us like to feel we have control of our lives. When we can make choices, we feel we have that control.

It's virtually impossible for you to develop a single exercise, project, case study, or activity that's exciting to every single person to whom you present it. By providing two, three, or even four activities and letting participants choose among them, you give them an opportunity to select something that creates a more personal motivational environment.

It's a peak experience to have in our programs eager, willing people who are there because they want to be, not because they have to be. We are not always so fortunate to have that learning environment created for us. But, by focusing on the preceding guidelines, we can improve the way we create an environment that produces better results from the training we deliver.

VISUAL AIDS

4

How to Keep Their Attention
When You Absolutely Have to Talk

WHY VISUAL AIDS?

Research has proven that it's possible to learn much more in a given period of time when visual aids are properly used. Studies at the University of Wisconsin have shown an improvement of up to 200 percent when vocabulary was taught using visual aids. Studies at Harvard and Columbia show between a 14 to 38 percent improvement in retention through the use of audiovisuals. And studies done at the University of Pennsylvania's Wharton School and at the University of Minnesota demonstrate clearly that the time required to present a concept was reduced up to 40 percent and the prospect of a favorable decision was greatly improved when visuals were used to augment a verbal presentation. Barriers of language, time, and space can be minimized by using appropriate audiovisuals.

Visual aids generally can be divided into two categories: projected and nonprojected. Projected visual aids include films, videotapes, slides, film strips, computer graphics, opaque projections, and overhead transparencies. Nonprojected visuals include pictures, posters, flip charts, flannel graphs, models, object lessons, simulators, maps, audiotapes, bulletin boards, chalk boards, and marker boards.

In his book *Presentations Plus,* David A. Peoples, a consulting instructor for IBM, says that people gain 75 percent of what they know visually, 13 percent through hearing, and a total of 12

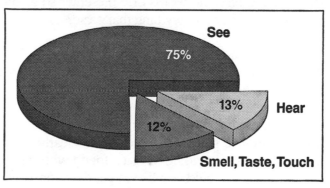

percent through smell, touch, and taste. A picture, he says, is three times more effective than words alone, and words and pictures together are six times more effective than words alone.

Clearly, there are some significant reasons for carefully designing and using visual aids. The ten most obvious reasons are these.

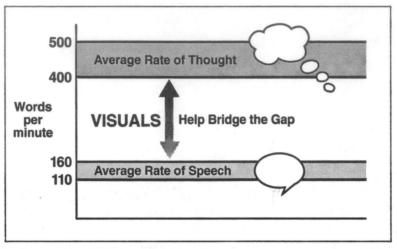

1. To Attract and Maintain Attention
The average individual speaks about 110 to 160 words per minute, but he or she thinks at a rate of 400 to 500 words per minute. Giving people visual stimulation can help keep them tied to the presentation rather than allowing their minds to wander elsewhere.

2. To Reinforce Main Ideas
We tend to put much more emphasis on what we see than on what we hear. If you don't believe that, recall the last time you saw a presentation where a visual was projected for which you did not have a handout. Wasn't there a tendency for you and for many of those around you to copy the information hurriedly before the visual was taken away? Yet how often do we hang onto the words of a presenter so attentively that we feel the need to write down everything that's said?

3. To Illustrate and Support the Spoken Word
The Chinese proverb says that a picture is worth a thousand words. But let's make that: A *well-chosen* picture or visual is worth a thousand words.

4. To Minimize Misunderstanding
Visuals can give meaning to words not clearly understood. Assume for a moment that you're going to visit a friend whose home you've never been to before. How would you like to get directions? Would you prefer simply to hear the instructions? Would you like the instructions written down? Or would you like a map? The importance of visuals becomes readily

apparent. Think about the last time you went to a shopping center or a mall and studied the building directory. How much easier it is to locate yourself and your destination when you see on the directory the little red dot that says "You are here" and the simple map that identifies the stores you want to visit.

5. To Increase Retention
Here's Confucius again: "What I hear, I forget; what I see, I remember; what I do, I understand." We have to remember something in order to be able to use it.

6. To Add a Touch of Realism
It may not be possible to have all the props, support materials, etc., that we would like in the classroom, but visuals can bring a welcome piece of the real world into an academic setting.

7. To Save Both Time and Money
Audiovisuals can help us communicate more clearly and quickly, so that participants understand the content we're trying to communicate.

8. To Aid in Organizing Your Thoughts
Audiovisuals can help us clarify our thinking and provide a logical path for communication.

9. To Ensure Covering Key Points
Not only do visuals give us a path to follow, they also ensure that we don't omit key points and that we cover them in the proper sequence.

10. To Build Confidence in Yourself
Knowing that you don't have to rely entirely on your memory for every facet of your presentation and knowing that your visuals are a "road map" that can guide you can help you to deliver your presentation with more confidence.

PROJECTED VISUALS

Films
Film is now going the way of the dinosaur. Yet these tips apply equally to videotape.

Films give you the advantage of showing motion, which is important for certain kinds of learning (for example, showing the steps involved in operating a machine). A film also can capture an event that you want to present as an illustration in a training program (for example, a sample interaction between a manager and an employee or a customer and a clerk).

Films require setup time and generally must be shown in a darkened room.

If you're going to use a film, choose it carefully and be sure to preview it. As you do, ask yourself these questions:

- Does it fit your needs?
- Will your audience perceive it as relevant?
- Is the language familiar and consistent with what your participants know, or does it require them to learn new terminology?
- Does it have direct application?
- Does the film come with listening guides, application activities, etc., that can help you integrate it into your learning process, or will you need to create these yourself?

A film is not simply an opportunity for a change of pace. It can and should be a significant learning activity that requires application. You don't want your participants tuning out when you turn on the projector. Pay careful attention to how you will introduce the film. Are there particular things you want your participants to look for? Perhaps it would be useful to break your participants into groups with each group looking for certain things; after the film, you can fully involve all your participants in a discussion of the various elements each group was looking for. Do you want to show the film in its entirety, or would it be useful to view parts of the film and then break away for discussion, application, etc., before going on to the rest of the film?

Equipment costs may dictate your use of films. The most commonly used film is the 16 millimeter (mm). Commercially produced films start at around $150 and can run up to $450 or more per copy. Films produced in-house can cost as much as $2500 per minute for color and $1700 for black and white. Good, used film projectors, such as the Bell and Howell Film-o-Sound, can be purchased for approximately $350. A new projector may cost as much as $2500.

Videotapes

Videotape can be used in much the same way as film, but it offers one advantage: it can be shown in a fully lit room.

Your playback system consists of a television monitor rather than a video projector. The rule of thumb I use is to have one diagonal inch of viewing screen for each participant. So, if I were running a training program with 25 participants, a 25-inch monitor (or two 19-inch monitors) would serve my purposes. Once I get beyond 75 people or so, it becomes more effective to use a video projector. But, again, costs can be a constraint. A 25-inch monitor can be purchased for between $300 and $500. A one-half inch VHS player/recorder can be purchased for as little as $200. But a video projector can run between $3000 and $7000. How often you're going to use the equipment can significantly affect the kind of investment you might be prepared to make. If you're going to use this medium infrequently and with large groups, it might be best to rent a video projector. Rental fees, depending upon your geographical location, can range anywhere from $75 a day to $400+ per day.

Videotape can also be used "real time" in the classroom. This can be especially useful if participants are doing a skill practice, such as giving a presentation or practicing a performance appraisal, closing a sale, or handling a customer complaint.

I like the model given to me by Bernie Birnbrauer and Lynn Tyson; we served together as faculty for an education forum for IBM's technical educators that was offered for graduate credit at Vanderbilt University. Rather than videotaping in front of the entire group of 35 to 40 participants, Bernie and Lynn formed work groups of approximately six participants and videotaped within these groups. Subgroups, or triads, were formed in each of the work groups. The process goes something like this.

1. A short presentation is given in front of the group of six, with five group members observing the presenter. Since each person has his or her own videotape, all presentations are on the same tape and can be kept afterwards for personal review and use. (I might add that presenters feel more secure when they know that the only permanent record of their presentation is in their own possession!)

2. During the presentation, each group member fills out a feedback sheet to give to the presenter later.

3. After the presentation, the participants meet in their subgroups.

4. In the subgroups, each participant cycles through three roles: mentor, student, and observer. Let's say, for example, that the three participants are Chris, Jan, and Lee. In the first round, Chris serves as mentor, Jan serves as student, and Lee as the observer. All three watch Jan's videotape. Chris, as a mentor, has a checklist of things to look for, and Lee has a mentor's checklist, too. After watching the videotape, Jan, as the student, has the first opportunity to debrief and identify the strengths and weaknesses of the presentation. After Jan's debriefing, Chris (as the mentor) would provide further feedback on the strengths and weaknesses of the presentation. Finally, Lee, as the observer, wraps up the process, giving feedback to Chris on how effectively Chris coached, or counseled, Jan. The three individuals would then rotate their roles, according to the following chart, until each had an opportunity to be mentor, student, and observer.

	MENTOR	STUDENT	OBSERVER
ROUND 1	Chris	Jan	Lee
ROUND 2	Lee	Chris	Jan
ROUND 3	Jan	Lee	Chris

A fourth member can be added to the group. The rotation would then look like this:

	MENTOR	STUDENT 1	STUDENT 2	OBSERVER
ROUND 1	Chris	Jan	Tim	Lee
ROUND 2	Lee	Chris	Jan	Tim
ROUND 3	Tim	Lee	Chris	Jan
ROUND 4	Jan	Tim	Lee	Chris

This method offers a number of advantages. First, it maximizes group participation. Each person gets an opportunity to practice the skill and receive feedback. Second, it enables the group to review and reinforce significant concepts several times without becoming bored. Even though each participant is going to view a number of presentations, the process stays fresh. In one case, a participant looks at the presentation through the eyes of someone who must provide feedback to the presenter; in another case, the participant assumes the role of an observer, looking not only for items to comment on but also considering the feedback from this altered position.

Another advantage is that the feedback is balanced. If I'm the mentor, I know that I'll be receiving feedback about my effectiveness as coach or counselor. This knowledge helps me follow the "Goldilocks approach" to coaching and counseling: not too hot, not too cold, just right or not too hard, not too soft, just right. Most of us, at one time or another, have received "Pollyanna" feedback, where we were praised so much we could hardly believe it was really justified. Perhaps each of us also has experienced the opposite, where someone comes down on us like a ton of bricks, and we wonder if criticism that severe was really justified either.

The drawback to the method just described is that it may not be cost effective. It does require a video camera, which can cost anywhere from $500 up, depending on quality, for each group of six. It requires a videotape recorder/player for each group of six or, preferably, for each group of three; this can cost anywhere from $200 on up. And it requires a television monitor, costing anywhere from $200 on up, for each group.

Videotape also can be used to create in-house presentations that can be used in much the same way as films. But before you make major video purchases, be sure you're going to use the equipment often enough and effectively enough to justify the expenditures. One of our clients, for whom we conduct a five-day train-the-trainer program once a year, thought the videotape feedback method was appropriate, but they realized they would only use the equipment this intensively once a year. They had two cameras, video recorders, and monitors in-house and discovered, through a little creative research, that they could rent monitors inexpensively for the week and that several course participants had cam-corders they could borrow. Thus, they were spared considerable expense.

Another option to consider is conducting your training in a hotel that has VCRs in the individual rooms. I conducted one four-day "Train the Trainer" session in an Embassy Suite because each VCR connected to the TV in the parlor. That enabled the participants to use the parlors as break-out rooms which saved us the expenses of renting VCRs and of providing additional break-out rooms.

You, too, might consider renting or borrowing the equipment before making a final purchase decision. Determine how frequently the equipment will be utilized and whether or not it will give you the results you desire. You may decide that, if you're going to use the equipment extensively and get the most out of it, you would have to invest either in outside experts (that is, video consultants) or add an internal staff that has the expertise to operate the equipment and to script and edit videotape.

Computer Graphics

Computer graphics are being used increasingly in business presentations as well as in the training room in a variety of ways. They can be developed and displayed on computer monitors. They can be used as an alternative to a slide presentation or even overhead transparencies. Programs such as PC Storyboard allow you to create visuals that can be displayed on a computer monitor in a sequence much like slides or film strips. They offer the additional advantage of providing some video-like effects, such as wipes, dissolves, and fades. They also can provide animation.

Computer graphics can be output from the computer into other types of presentation media. The use of additional equipment such as a Polaroid Palette can allow you to create 35mm slides from the computer graphics you've designed. These graphics also can be output as hard copy, to be used as handouts, particularly if you have access to a laser-jet printer. They can output into color transparencies, using either a color plotter or a color printer.

Depending on the equipment you have, your computer graphics also can be incorporated into videotapes. They can be displayed either in color or monochrome on the overhead projector, using display systems such as Kodak's Datashow or Proxima's Ovation. This allows you to take information that would show up on a computer screen and project it via an overhead projector to a large audience. It can be displayed to a larger audience using larger monitors or video projectors.

General Parametrics offers even more sophisticated uses for computer graphics. Its VideoShow system lets you create and display computer graphics in a choice of over 256,000 colors at five times the resolution of an IBM PC. Several computer graphics programs (such as Freelance Plus, Harvard Graphics, and Picture It) and clip art libraries (such as the Freelance Library and Picture Paks from Imageline) offer resources that you can use to create extremely high-powered visuals. These visuals are created on an IBM-compatible computer and then displayed through the VideoShow system, either on television monitors or video projectors. It is also possible to output these high-resolution computer graphics as slides or color transparencies (or hard copy for handouts).

Assuming that you already have a computer, you may discover that the use of computer graphics is not as expensive or as difficult to incorporate as you thought. The software necessary to create computer graphics can run from as little as zero dollars—for graphics packages that can be picked up from public-domain bulletin boards—to very complete packages in the $495-and-up range. If you want to add graphics to your visuals and also have the option of using them in your handouts, you should certainly explore this area.

In the appendix, you'll find a summary of several graphics packages you can use for creating your own graphics.

35mm Slides

Slides are probably the most common still pictures used in training and other types of presentations. The carousel projector, which typically holds 80 slides in a circular tray, is frequently found in training departments. Some versions of the round slide tray hold up to 120 slides, but users may find they trade off dependability for the larger number of slides; jamming can occur as slides begin to age and slide mounts warp. When purchasing a projector, make sure it will handle easily the type of slide you plan to use. 35mm slides can be mounted in plastic, cardboard, metal, or glass frames. A projector should be sturdy, reliable, and relatively quiet to operate. An additional useful feature is a remote-control device.

Typically, slide projectors still require an almost completely darkened room. This presents a couple of disadvantages. It may be difficult to change trays in the dark. And, depending on the time of day, some participants may nod off when the lights go down.

If you're going to use your slide projector in a variety of locations, consider purchasing a zoom lens. This will allow you to position your projector strategically and then use the lens both to focus and adjust the size of your pictures so they fill the screen.

Opaque Projectors

With opaque projectors, you can project solid materials, such as drawings, magazine photographs, etc., without turning them into overhead transparencies. It's a good process to use if you have to display and discuss intricate diagrams. It can also be effective in projecting material from which you would like to make charts; you can trace this material onto flip-chart paper and then keep it for later use.

Overhead Projectors

Overhead projectors are probably the most widely used machines in the projector category. The room can be fairly well-lit while an overhead projector is being used. This allows the instructor to face the class and also to alter the visual as the discussion develops.

INSIDER'S TIP

Whenever possible, use an overhead projector that has the light source underneath the stage. It eliminates the double image sometimes created by overhead projectors with the light source in the head that reflects off a mirror on the stage. The light passes through the transparency twice in the mirror system. If you use overlays that don't lie entirely flat, it can create a blurred or double-image effect.

Transparencies for the overhead projector are also fairly easy to make, as well as being inexpensive.

NONPROJECTED VISUALS

Pictures

Pictures can be effective visual aids, particularly in such presentations as orientation programs—where you want to provide an overall view of a company and its various divisions and components. If you're describing new machinery, equipment, products, etc., large pictures mounted on foam board (which then can be placed on permanent display) are very effective.

Posters

Almost every training program lends itself to some key concepts that can be captured on a poster board. Posters can be particularly effective for presentations that you're giving several times. Guidelines for the use of other permanent visual aids apply here as well. Posters can be used effectively in conjunction with other visual aids.

I also use posters when I introduce what I call the Funnel Concept. Our poster shows a funnel with the word "unknown" above it. Beneath the unknown we have a number of prospects. Those prospects tend to filter through the funnel. To the right of the funnel are the words "prospecting," "appointments," "presentations," "enrollments," and "referrals." There are holes in this funnel, indicating that some prospects are eliminated at the prospecting stage. That is, they never become an appointment. Others are cancelled at the appointment stage. That is, the appointment cancels and you never make a presentation, etc. Some prospects come out the bottom of the funnel as sales. Again, after I explain the concept, the poster remains on display in front of the group.

As another example, in one seminar I do, I introduce what I call the Sales Success, or PAPER, Cycle, which consists of these key points:

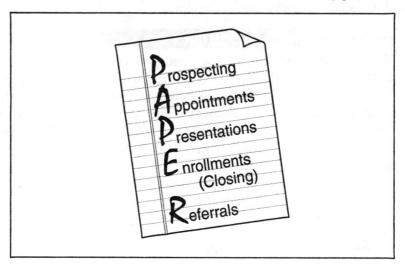

I had a sign painter depict the following cycle, in five different colors, on foam board. When I first present the concept in the seminar, I use a transparency to relate the points and build the cycle, with an arrow going clockwise from "prospecting." I continue to add arrows around the circle until I reach "referrals," which points back to the first step, "prospecting." After we've discussed the basic transparency, I reveal the permanent poster to the audience so they can refer to it for the rest of the seminar.

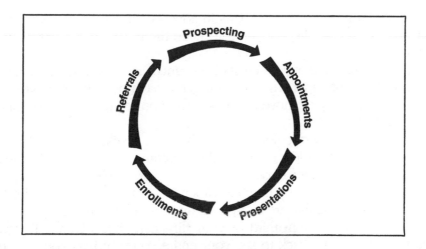

Chalk and White Magnetic Marker Boards

The marker board is the modern-day version of the chalk board, and each can be effective in communicating information to participants. Markers come in a wide variety of colors. Many marker boards are magnetized, so items can be affixed to them with magnets.

If you are presenting basic concepts with a magnetic board, print key words on show cards with magnetic strips attached. Then, simply place the signs on the magnetic board wherever you want them. I frequently use this technique in seminars when we're building upon concepts. As each idea is presented, it's placed on the magnetic board so participants can see how the concepts relate to one another.

Flip Charts

Flip charts are widely used—and misused—in the training process. They can be used effectively to create real-time visuals (that is, they're drawn as the presentation takes place), or they can be developed in advance.

Basically, flip charts are suitable only if your group is relatively small, 15 to 20 people at the most. People sitting in the back of a larger group have trouble seeing flip charts.

We already have discussed the preparation of overheads and slides; many of the same rules apply to flip charts.

Here are some simple tips that can increase the effectiveness of a flip chart.

1. If you have basic points to make, pencil them in lightly on your various sheets of chart paper before the presentation. Then you can use your markers to write in the words so everybody can see them. In a sense, your chart paper becomes a very large set of notes or an outline.

2. Prepare some of your charts in advance, and simply overlay them with two or three sheets of paper to keep them from being prematurely visible.

3. Prepare some of your charts in advance, and cover the basic points with cut strips of paper. Then, as you get to each point in your presentation, you can simply remove the paper strip you've taped over that particular point on the chart.

4. Use a variety of colors beyond the basic black, red, and blue that we so often see. Consider not using these common colors at all. Try bright colors that people aren't used to seeing. For example, I use design-art markers, manufactured by Eberhart-Faber, in such colors as red-violet and blue-green—colors that are easily seen and just a bit unusual.

5. Leave the bottom third of your flip-chart sheets blank. This will allow people in the back to see your entire page, and, as you post flip charts on the wall, it leaves space to go back and add more information.

6. Brighten the chart's visual appeal. You can do this by underlining or boxing key words. Use color, graphic designs, and geometric shapes to add visual interest to your chart.

7. Use flip-chart pages to record information. For example, during a brainstorming session, write key words that reflect each contributor's ideas. Better still, have two or three participants record on flip charts ideas as they come up. This allows you to maintain control of the group, clarify ideas, etc., while someone else does the writing. Give participants who will be recording material two different-colored markers, and ask them to alternate colors as the ideas are presented.

Remember the Four T's of flip charts.

1. **T**urn to the flipchart as you address information on it and stand to the side as you're discussing the information.

2. **T**ouch the information that you're talking about. You may have three or four items listed on the flip chart. Touch the particular item that you are talking about or use a moveable keynote that you can place next to the item under discussion and then move it as you move to another item.

3. **T**ear off the flip chart when you have finished using it. Don't simply flip it over to the back. If the ideas have value, tear it off.

4. **T**ape it to the wall so that that information can serve as an ongoing reminder of content. This is one distinct value the flip chart has over other types of visual aids.

Flannel Graphs

Flannel graphs, in their original form, probably remind at least some people of Sunday School lessons; as the teacher told a bible story, he or she placed on a piece of flannel board cloth cut-outs representing various characters. Today, we still see flannel graphs used; as the presentation unfolds, additional elements are placed on the flannel graph.

Models

Models can be effective hands-on visual aids. These might be miniature representations of something too large to be brought into the classroom. Most models are static representations of real objects. They can range from miniatures of cars, pumps, and other machines to houses and skyscrapers, complete with removable cutaways to show key parts of the exterior. While most models are small representations of the real thing, some can be larger. For example, Saudia Airlines has the only "larger than life" instrument panel for a Boeing 747 jet. Used to train pilots, it is five times larger than the actual panel on the plane. Operating exactly like the real thing, it allows each member of a class of 20 to see clearly. The instructor can use a model for demonstration, and participants can practice new skills on a model.

Sometimes a model is an actual piece of equipment. Make sure your models are realistic. A friend of mine once participated in a training program that taught mechanics to break down and repair a transmission. The models used in the classroom were elegantly designed, with various parts color-coded. By the end of the training program, the participants could readily disassemble and assemble the transmission. They could identify the parts not only by location and function but also by color. Unfortunately, when they went on to the actual shop floor, they had to look at the transmission from underneath, not from on top as they had been able to do in the training room. And, obviously, none of the transmissions they attempted to repair was color-coded. They would have learned more by working on real, greasy transmissions that they could have seen from all angles than they learned by working on pristine classroom models.

Simulators

Simulators are mock-ups of the real thing. They can be as simple as a counter with a cash register that simulates a store environment or as complex as a replica of a 747 cockpit that costs millions of dollars and duplicates (through the use of interactive video, videodisk technology, and highly complex and sophisticated electro-mechanical systems) exactly what it is like to fly a 747 jet. Simulators effectively bring into the classroom realistic imitations of things that are otherwise unavailable.

Objects

Tangible objects can be used to teach a lesson. For example, I've used children's puzzles to help demonstrate competition versus collaboration. I've used potatoes and straws to demonstrate the need to follow through.

And I've used cookies to help participants recall the fun of learning that most of us experienced in kindergarten, where a favorite activity was our cookies-and-milk break.

WHAT MAKES A GOOD VISUAL?

As you prepare your presentation, ask these seven questions to determine the effectiveness of every visual aid you use.

1. Is the Visual Clear?

Is it obvious, at a glance, what the visual you are using is trying to communicate?

2. Is It Readable?

Can people actually SEE the information, or is the material so complex or the printing so tiny that it's not visible to most of your audience?

3. Does the Visual Communicate a Single Idea?

Is your audience able to focus on one key point, as you expand on your visual, or are their thoughts cluttered because more than one idea is presented?

4. Is It Relevant?

Does the audience know why you're using the visual? Does it make a point that fits in with the presentation?

5. Is It Interesting?

Does it help focus and keep the audience's attention?

6. Is It Simple?

Is it easy for the audience to relate to the visual, or is it so busy, so detailed, so cluttered with graphics, so colorful, so full of various typefaces that it is difficult to focus on?

7. Is It Accurate?

Does it clearly portray what it's meant to portray? For example, the diagram at the top of the following page illustrates two visuals that convey the same information. The first one shows the bar chart truncated, so that the difference between the two bars does not seem significant. The second visual clearly shows the difference between the two bars. Some will argue that you need to save space and that it's not proportional, etc. But if we're going to be accurate, the audience must see at a glance the vast difference in the two bars.

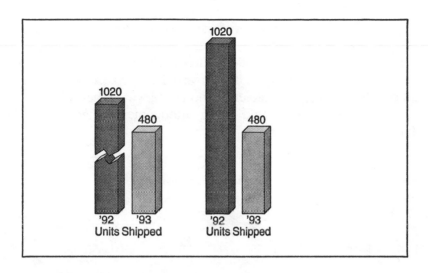

PREPARING THE ROOM AND EQUIPMENT

Projected Visuals

Whenever you're going to use projected visuals, you must carefully plan, in advance, where to locate your projector (whether 16mm, video, overhead, opaque, or slide projector). Though these guidelines may be most appropriate for the overhead projector, nearly all apply to all projected visuals. The point is simple: Make sure each person in the audience can see every visual you use.

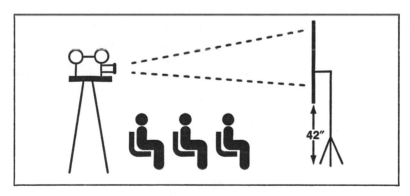

1. Each person should be able to see the screen easily.

The bottom of the screen should be at least 42 inches off the floor. This height is higher than the tops of the heads of 95 percent of your seated audience.

2. For best visibility, place the screen in a corner and angle it toward the center of the room.

This is particularly true for overhead and opaque projectors, but it applies to other visual projectors as well. You don't want a large, blank screen to be the center of attention when you're not using a projected visual. If you choose to write on certain visuals, this placement allows you to do so while facing your audience and not blocking their view.

Here are some suggested room arrangements that can facilitate visibility.

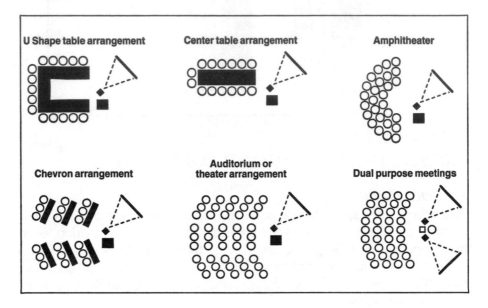

You'll notice the chevron is similar to classroom style, but it permits participants to see one another. The auditorium and dual projector arrangements feature seating in an arc for the same purpose.

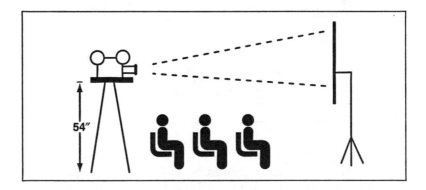

3. Your projector should not obstruct your audience's view of the screen.

If you're using a 16mm or 35mm projector, place it on a stand so the audience has an unobstructed view of the entire visual. Special lenses are available that permit you to place the projector all the way at the back of the room on a high stand (normally 54″ high) and project over the heads of your seated participants. If you're using an overhead projector, which is placed in front of your participants, make sure it does not block your participants' view. Place an overhead projector on a surface large enough to hold at least two stacks of visuals and other equipment and props you may use in your presentation. This arrangement allows you to move prepared visuals from stack A, those you haven't used yet, to stack B, those already used.

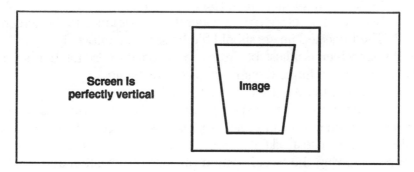

4. Avoid image distortion or "keystoning" by having the projector beam meet the center of the screen at a 90 degree angle.

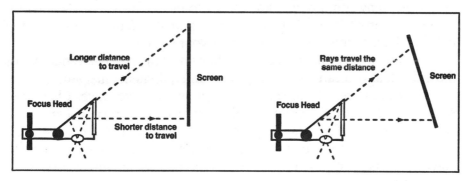

Keystoning occurs when the projector is placed low, in order to keep it out of the audience's line of vision. It is caused by the difference between the distances that bottom and top rays of light have to travel between the focus and the screen. The farther the ray of light has to travel, the wider the image. You can avoid this effect by tilting the screen forward at the top or backward at the bottom so that the distances traveled by the various rays are about the same at all points on the screen.

5. Whenever possible, use a matte surface screen for greatest image visibility and seating breadth.

Beaded (or lenticular) screens reflect more light to viewers in the center of the room, but the image dulls and drops off when viewed from the sides of the room. A beaded screen is fine if you have a long, narrow room, but a matte screen will serve you best in most situations.

6. To select the right screen size and seating arrangements, remember the two-by-six rule.

• The distance from the screen from the first row of seats should equal twice the width of the screen (2w).

• The distance from the screen to the last row of seats should equal six times the width of the screen (6w).

• No row of seats should be wider than its distance to the screen.

7. The projected image should fill the screen completely.

If your screen is adjustable from top to bottom, raise the bottom of the screen in order to frame the image you're projecting.

8. Always carry extra accessories.

An extension cord, three-pronged plug adapter, masking tape, marking pens (for an overhead projector), blank sheets of write-on film, spare projector bulbs: The availability of these "spares" may mean the difference between showing the visual portion of your presentation and not being able to.

9. Know the room you're going to use.

Know the location of light switches, electrical outlets, and heating and air-conditioning controls, and know how to use them. Which light switch do you use in order to darken the room partially? Can you turn off the lights in the area immediately in front of your screen?

10. Know the location of the telephone and the name and number of the individual you can contact in case of an equipment emergency.

11. Set up and check out your equipment in advance. Check the screen for keystoning. Test and focus the projector. If you're using sound, check the levels. If you're using an overhead projector, clean the glass stage of the projector with a soft cloth and water or lens cleaner. Tape any cords to the floor. Know how to change your projector lamp if necessary.

12. Check your visuals.

Make sure that they're numbered, right side up, in the proper sequence, and that they're clean and ready to use.

13. Make sure the air vent on your projector is clear.

If it's blocked, the lamp will overheat and burn out sooner.

14. Check your projector and screen placement by drawing sight lines at the top and bottom of the screen for both the audience (being careful to allow the sight line to extend over the heads of people seated in the front rows) and for the projector itself.

15. If you're going to use a back-of-the-room projector, you may want someone else to operate it for you.

If it's a slide projector, avoid having to say "Next slide, please" by giving the projectionist a copy of your presentation. Underline the words you'll use as cues for changing the slides, and rehearse these with your projectionist. Alternatively, you might give your projectionist a visual cue, such as touching the knot of your tie or your necklace. Make sure you and the projectionist know what to do if a slide jams, the film breaks, or something goes wrong with the videotape.

16. Clean the lens of the projector.

17. For larger rooms, consider a high-intensity projector that will project lots of light over a large distance to a large screen.

18. Short focal-length lenses can be used to produce a large image on a screen from a short projection distance.

This is useful for viewing large, impressive images in a shallow, wide room.

19. Long focal-length lenses can be used to produce small images or in places where long projection distances are required for relatively small images.

20. To facilitate viewing, seat people in a fan-shaped area of about 70 degrees with the center perpendicular to the screen.

Picking a Room

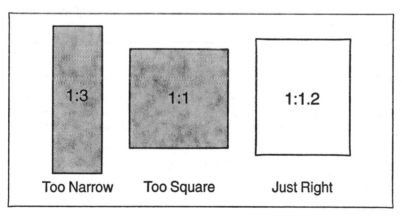

Whenever possible, hold your meeting in a room appropriate to the size of your group. If, however, you have a choice between a room that's a little too small and one that's a little too large, select the latter. There are ways to make a too-large room look smaller and cozier, but there's nothing you can do about overcrowding. The ideal room ratio is 1 foot of width to 1.2 feet of length. For most meetings, 12 to 20 square feet should be allowed per person.

Know the room layout so you can determine the best placement of people. You'll want to arrange it so your audience has enough room and your equipment is protected from being knocked around.

Seating

Be sure the chairs are comfortable; uncomfortable chairs can decrease your audience's attention span. Whenever possible, get chairs with arm-rests. Do you have enough chairs and tables for the number of participants you're expecting? Are the exits to the room clear once the room setup is complete?

Make sure that your meeting room has the exit at the rear of the room to minimize the distractions due to latecomers. Always set 10% fewer chairs than you think you're going to need, but have extras at the back of the room. It is much more energizing to be adding chairs than to start a session with too many chairs.

Screen Viewing

Avoid or minimize any obstructing posts or columns that interfere with visibility either of the speaker or the group members. Everybody should be able to see clearly when seated.

INSIDER'S TIP

Avoid placing an aisle in the center of your audience. The center offers the best seating for viewing, so place the aisle to either side.

Lighting

Make sure the room is well-lit but not so bright that the lights distract your listeners with glare. The room should be dark enough for projection yet light enough for note-taking. Check to see if the lights can be dimmed or switched independently. If not, can the light bulbs immediately in front of your screen be removed in order to darken the area around the screen? Use incandescent lights with dimming systems if possible. Check and label all light switches, and assign a person to turn lights on and off on cue. Light sources that create flicker can cause distraction and discomfort.

Power

Are electrical outlets adequate and conveniently located? How much extension cord will you need to bring power to your equipment? You should know if the current is AC or DC. Will it run your equipment? If you haven't brought an adapter with you, you may have problems with two- or three-pronged plugs that don't match up to the outlets. How much electricity will your meeting require? Overloading the line running to your meeting room will bring your class to a halt.

Check to see if outlets are switched and fused separately from the room lights and if spare fuses and standby circuit breakers are ready. An electrical outlet should be located near the head table to permit plugging in any equipment used by the speaker.

Acoustics

Bouncing sound waves get on the nerves of speakers and listeners, so check acoustics by clapping your hands together slowly. A brittle, ringing echo indicates poor acoustics. If you have this problem, you can reduce the bouncing sound waves by draping walls with fabric, placing carpeting on floors, or, if possible, finishing floors and ceiling with acoustic tiles.

Be sure that sound carries to all parts of the room. "Dead spots" can occur and can distract people from your message by making it difficult for them to hear. Make sure, also, that there is no interference from noisy mechanical equipment (e.g., projectors) placed too close to participants. Check to be sure that no loud sounds from outside the room will distract your class.

PREPARING TRANSPARENCIES

1. Limit your work area on the original to a maximum of eight-by-ten inches. This will ensure that, once your visual is prepared, you'll have room to mount and project it without having the framing block part of the visual.

2. Limit each visual to one idea.

If the topic you're covering is more complex, you might want to use overlays. You can superimpose additional transparencies on top of a base transparency to build a concept or progressively present a complex issue.

3. Keep your visuals as simple as possible.

Excessive wording or too-elaborate diagrams on a single visual not only compete with you, they become more and more difficult for the audience to read. Remember the six-by-six rule: No more than six lines per transparency and no more than six words on a line.

4. Use appropriate type sizes.

- Use at least 18-point type (1/4-inch-high letters) or more on visuals.
- Use bold, simple typefaces.
- Avoid ornate styles for maximum readability.
- Vary the type size in order to illustrate the relative importance of information.
- Never use a typewriter to create your masters.
- Use the same type style for each series of transparencies.

• Use upper- and lower-case letters. Lower case are generally more legible than upper case. Occasionally use only upper case for contrast or for headings.

• Vary the length of words and provide ample spacing between the letters, between the words, and between the lines of type. A good guideline: Between each line of type, leave a space equal to the height of an upper-case letter of the size and style you are using.

Plan Approach

A. Gain Attention

B. Introduce Lesson

C. Transitions

The words are clear in this illustration but there is no visual impact.

Plan Approach

A. Gain Attention

B. Introduce Lesson

C. Transitions

The words are the same but now the plane landing (on approach) provides VISUAL reinforcement.

---

5. Be imaginative.

Use illustrations, cartoons, graphs, maps, and charts whenever possible, instead of relying exclusively upon words or numbers.

6. Use tinted film to reduce lamp wear and colored markings to add realism and emphasis.

Tinted films also can provide a means for color coding your transparencies. You might use the same tint for a series of transparencies on one topic, then change the background tint for another topic.

7. Use the space on your transparencies to make ad lib markings during your presentation.

8. Position your material on the upper part of your transparency. When you project it, your audience can view it readily since it will be on the top part of the screen.

9. Avoid using both horizontal and vertical forms.

Many experts suggest using horizontal visuals exclusively for maximum visibility.

<table>
<tr><td>

1. Give people the SAFETY to be who they are.
2. Give them the FREEDOM to be what they are.
3. Give UNCONDITIONALLY your full attention.

</td><td>

1. Give SAFETY.
2. Give FREEDOM.
3. Give FULL ATTENTION.

</td></tr>
<tr><td>

More words reduce the size of type that can be used. This visual is okay by most guidelines, but from a textual standpoint could be clearer by using key words only.

</td><td>

Here's the same basic visual, but the concept is clearer because the message is conveyed by key words. The speaker can then expand on the points to be made rather than just reading the text being projected.

</td></tr>
</table>

10. Choose your words carefully.

When creating visuals, try to think in "bullets." Use active words and short phrases.

11. Use—but don't overuse—color.

A maximum of two to three colors per transparency should be sufficient. More than that will make it difficult for the eye to focus on the important parts of the visual.

12. Avoid vertical lettering.

A quick look at these two visuals shows the importance of this suggestion. Vertical lettering may look fancy, but it's very difficult to read.

Don't use more than two type styles.

Don't use more than two type styles.

Don't use more than two type styles.

Don't use more than two type styles.

Don't use more than two type styles.

13. Use a maximum of two type styles on any single visual.

Any more than two causes the type styles to compete with the information being presented.

14. If you're using nonsequential items in a visual, don't number the items. Use check marks, bullets, boxes, arrows, etc.

15. Clip-art books can be a great source of copyright-free illustrations, giving you inexpensive, ready-made professional art.

A HIGH-IMPACT GRAPHIC TECHNIQUE

Window Paning

We've already stated that the mind thinks in pictures. Pictures can also be used to help people retain ideas much more quickly and with much more permanency. Back in the 1930s, AT&T did research in setting up local phone numbers. As you know, in the United States, phone numbers are seven digits, grouped in three digits first, followed by four digits and followed by a hyphen. This is known as chunking. Based on research, they found that a person could retain in short term memory seven bits of information plus or minus two. This is one reason that the phone number has seven digits.

Many of us have had the experience of looking up a phone number in the phone book, dialing it, having it be busy and then having to look it up again because as soon as we dialed it we pushed it out of short term memory—it was not stored in long term memory for recall. The mind thinks in pictures, so if we take the AT&T idea, it says that we can create an array of pictures to help people remember. This is a techniques we call "Window Paning." For example, look at the window pane that we've given here. It's a two-by-six matrix. The first picture, a computer, represents the fact that training directors of the '90s are concerned about the technology explosion and how they keep people up-to-date with it. The pair of ballerina slippers in square two indicate that training directors are concerned with balancing needs of the individual with the needs of the organization. The book, turning into a floppy disk, represents the concern the training directors have for the information explosion. Knowledge is doubling about every 18 months—how will they keep up with people's need for information. The egg cracking open with the star coming out of it in window four represents the training directors' concern for finding, hatching, and growing their superstars—the people who can react with the dynamic and rapid change that the organization will experience. Window pane five, the person inside prison with the universal "Do Not" sign, represents the training directors' concern for retaining good employees without having them feel as if they're in prison. And finally, window pane six represents the training directors' concern with having to downsize when it's needed, and yet be balanced in paying attention to the concerns to the individuals and the communities affected.

Six window panes, and six critical pieces of information that are much easier to retain by being able to recall the pictures which give us the concept than if we had simply presented with a traditional list such as you find below. Here are the six greatest concerns for training directors of the 1990s based on an ASTD study published in January of 1991.

1. The technology explosion.

2. The need to balance the needs of the individual with the needs of the organization.

3. The information explosion and the fact that information is doubling every 18 months.

4. How do we find, hatch, and grow our superstars who can react to the dynamic change that's going to be happening in the organization?

5. How do we retain good employees without having them feel as if they're in prison?

6. How do we downsize when it's necessary, and yet balance the needs of the individuals and communities who are going to be affected?

It's much simpler for people to recall the pictures that trigger the concepts than to memorize the words or somehow be able to recall the words that represent the concept itself. So whenever you're creating visuals, remember that graphics aid retention. If you've got a series of points, consider using the window pane to display them graphically. This gives people not only a picture, but also a physical location that the picture is placed in. It also means that if you've got a series of steps to be followed, it makes it much easier to become aware of which step might have been missed.

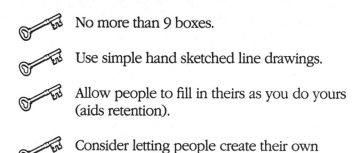

KEYS FOR WINDOW PANING

No more than 9 boxes.

Use simple hand sketched line drawings.

Allow people to fill in theirs as you do yours (aids retention).

Consider letting people create their own window panes.

REPRODUCING YOUR TRANSPARENCIES

1. For neat, free-hand lettering, place a piece of graph paper under the film as a lettering guide. Or use acetate sheets with etched grid lines.

2. Use projectable, colored, adhesive-backed sheets to fill large areas of color. Adding color with transparency markers can be done with small dots or slanted lines; avoid the uneven appearance of overlapped strokes that result when you "color" in an area with markers.

3. To protect your transparencies, sandwich them between two pieces of clear acetate. That way you can mark on the acetate without affecting your original.

4. Masking allows you to reveal elements of a transparency either progressively or selectively.

- You can use any opaque material for masking. Onion skin or a white opalescent plastic sheet lets you see covered elements through the mask.

- For progressive disclosure, slide the mask off the image to expose the visual gradually.

- For selective disclosure, cut the mask into sections and tape or hinge them to the mount. Lift appropriate pieces to reveal different portions of the visual. (You may want to number the mask sections in the order they are to be presented.)

Mounting Your Transparencies

Mount your transparencies with plastic or paperboard frames. Mounting serves several purposes. It helps you manipulate your visuals, prevents acetate from curling, provides you with space for notes and ID codes, and blocks the broad band of projected light that results when a transparency is smaller than the stage aperture.

Mounting your transparencies is easy. Simply center the transparency face down over the back of the mount and tape all four edges to the frame.

INSIDER'S TIP

Place sheets of paper between your transparencies. This aids in reading and protecting each transparency. And, it can be used to block out light by leaving a sheet of paper under the transparency as you place it on the overhead projector. Then, remove it when you're ready for participants to view it.

To mount overlays, use the following procedure.

1. Mount one or more base transparencies face down on the back of the mount.

2. Superimpose and tape each overlay face up on the front of the mount.

3. Then fasten overlays to the same edge or on different edges for flexible sequencing.

4. Make sure the tape doesn't run past the edges of the overlays to assure smooth hinging action.

To mount multicolor transparencies, use the following procedure.

1. Center and tape the base transparency face down over the back of the mount.

2. Superimpose each color sheet over the base, making sure the registration is accurate, and then fasten.

3. Cover with a second frame, and tape the edges of the two mounts together.

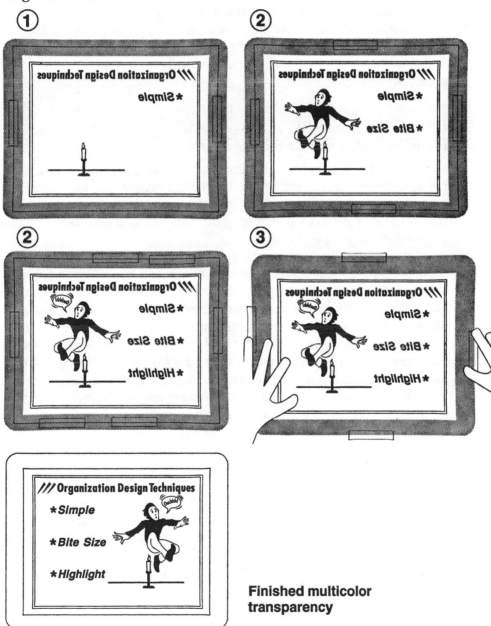

Finished multicolor transparency

There are alternatives to mounting.

• *Flip Frames*, by 3M Company of St. Paul, Minnesota, provide a transparent sleeve to contain your transparency. The frame then "flips" into place, eliminating any extra light from your projection area.

• *Flipatran*, by Visual Systems of Milwaukee, Wisconsin, lets you display and store 30 transparencies in a single volume. Each transparency flips into view on the overhead projector and then can be flipped out of the way, making room for the next transparency.

• *Instraframe*, available from Resources for Organizations, Inc., of Edina, Minnesota, is an injection-molded frame with a glass stage that instantly frames your visual and keeps it properly centered on the overhead projector.

USING TRANSPARENCIES DURING YOUR PRESENTATION

Very simple techniques can significantly affect your presentation of visuals. For instance, by turning the lamp on and off at appropriate times, you can control your audience's attention. Keep the lamp off when changing visuals; you won't have to look at lamp glare, and your audience won't be distracted if positioning is clumsy.

If the objective is to block the light but not turn it off, there are other alternatives. One is to place a sheet of paper or a file folder trimmed to size underneath your visual. Slide the sheet down to reveal information, and, when you're finished, slide it back into place on the projector stage to block the light while you're positioning the next slide.

Another alternative is to tape a six-by-six-inch piece of cardboard to the projector head so you can flip it out of the way when you want to project an image and flip it down when you want to block the light.

If you add detail to a transparency during the presentation, use nonpermanent markers or write on a clear sheet of film placed over the prepared visual, so you can use the original again.

If an assistant is changing the visuals, determine in advance a system of signals so this individual knows exactly when to change the transparencies without your audience having to hear you call for each new one. Once again, it is important that the visuals be clean, in the correct order, right side up, and facing the correct direction *before* your class starts.

Be careful not to obstruct the projector light beam if you move around the room during a presentation.

If a transparency is to be used repeatedly, make copies for projection and store the master. When your copies begin to wear, you can use the master to make additional copies.

Keep blank sheets of film beside the projector so you can ad lib on your visuals.

And, remember, having a spare lamp (or, if possible, a spare projector) on hand can save a lot of grief during your presentation.

Consider the following guidelines before you select the appropriate method(s) for preparing your transparencies.

DIRECT PROCESSES

Direct simply means you're going to create the visual by writing directly on the transparency itself.

Method: Grease pencils
Equipment: Grease pencils
Relative time: Short to moderate
Expense: Low
Comments: Projects jet black or subdued colors; easy to use; erases with dry cloth; pencil doesn't hold fine point; apt to smear

Method: Marking pens
Equipment: Marking pens (permanent or nonpermanent)
Relative time: Short to moderate
Expense: Low
Comments: Quick and easy; can produce thin lines or bold strokes; bright colors

Method: Dry transfer letters
Equipment: Dry transfer letters
Relative time: Moderate
Expense: Moderate
Comments: Available in various styles and sizes; mistakes can be removed with masking tape; can be expensive if visual requires much lettering

Method: Lettering templates
Equipment: Lettering templates
Relative time: Moderate
Expense: Low
Comments: Available in many styles and sizes; produces uniform letter size

Method: Graphic tapes
Equipment: Graphic tapes
Relative time: Short
Expense: Moderate
Comments: Pressure-sensitive; quick and easy; limited applications, but good for outlines, charts, graphs; available in variety of colors, widths, patterns; opaque or transparent

INDIRECT PROCESSES (NO SIZE CHANGE)

Method: Spirit duplicator
Equipment: Spirit duplicator, frosted or matte acetate, clear plastic spray
Relative time: Short
Expense: Moderate
Comments: Produces good, solid, dark line work; good for making simple transparencies (single or multicolor) or multiple paper copies; requires care when feeding into machine and when spraying

Method: Diazo
Equipment: Diazo film, ultra-violet light printer, chamber of ammonia vapor
Relative time: Moderate
Expense: Moderate
Comments: Film can be processed in ordinary room light; produces brilliant colors; minimal fade or discoloration; base of original must be translucent or transparent, and markings must be opaque; good for line drawings, letters, and continuous tone images; can be used for variety of applications; relatively complex process requiring skill

Method: Thermal
Equipment: Infra-red-light copy machine, thermal film
Relative time: Very short
Expense: Moderate
Comments: All markings on original must contain carbon; heat destroys backing of transfer letters and paste-up art; use of several different marking devices may cause uneven line density; good for one-color transparencies; a photocopy of the original should be used as the master for duplication

Method: Picture lift
Equipment: Adhesive-backed clear acetate or shelf paper
Relative time: Short to moderate
Expense: Moderate
Comments: Cheapest way to transfer full-color pictures to transparency; original must be printed on clay-coated paper; destroys the original; can also be done with laminating machine or dry-mount press; very few applications

INDIRECT PROCESSES (WITH SIZE CHANGE)

Method: Electrostatic
Equipment: Xerographic or electrostatic copy machine, special film
Relative time: Very short
Expense: Low
Comments: Fast, clean; fair quality; degree of density of copy depends on colors of original markings and background; best for line subjects; permits quick transfer from printed page to acetate; yields poor-quality photos and half tones; size change requires a copy machine that will reduce or enlarge the original

Method: Photographic
Equipment: Camera and darkroom
Relative time: Long
Expense: Moderate to high
Comments: Requires skill, complex and costly equipment; produces high-quality transparencies

PRODUCING AND USING SLIDES

Many of the basic guidelines for production and effective use of overhead transparencies, including design and layout, can be applied directly to the use of 35mm slides. If you're going to use slides instead of overhead transparencies, consider the following 18 basic guidelines.

1. Edit slides beforehand to make sure you have the right ones, that they are in sequence, and that none is upside down or the wrong way around.

2. Decide if you want horizontal, vertical, or mixed slides. This affects the screen size and projected image size. In most cases, horizontal-format slides (slides that are wider than they are high) should be used, because most screens are wider than they are high. Vertical slides or a mix of vertical and horizontal slides are better used on a square screen.

3. Design slides for the back row.

4. For average back-row viewing distances, large letter height is advised. A maximum of five to six words per line and a maximum of five lines of copy per slide are good general rules of thumb. To determine maximum viewing distance, use eight times the height of the projected image.

5. For maximum effect, use ten or fewer words per slide.

6. To make sure your lettering is of readable height, have letters measure one-quarter inch on the finished slide.

7. Use strong, bold sans serif typefaces for reading ease. Don't use all upper-case letters. Provide ample spacing between words and letters.

8. Choose simple words. Use active words and short sentences, and write in conversational style (write for listening). Words should reinforce visuals.

9. Make sure slides are clean. There are several commercial cleaning products available.

10. Make slides crisp and dynamic.

11. Rehearse your presentation.

12. Use illustrations, cartoons, and drawings whenever possible.

13. Make good use of color contrast. Use a dark blue, black, or brown background. Use white, yellow, or red for the letters and pictures.

14. Use a remote-control projector, or have an assistant change slides so you can face the audience as much as possible.

15. Mark the forward button on the remote switch with white tape. This prevents going backwards and makes it easier to locate in a darkened room.

16. Start and end with a black slide so you won't shock the audience with blinding lights.

17. Depending on the type of projector used, mount slides in plastic or in metal and glass holders. Cardboard-mounted slides tend to bend and may jam the slide tray.

18. Limit the number of slides to the time available. Figure on 15 to 20 seconds per slide.

SUMMARY

Remember, visuals are instruments used in presenting a message, but they are not the message itself. Select your visual materials with care, aiming for simplicity and choosing the easiest and most effective transmission system. Familiarize yourself with the equipment you will use. A few minutes spent with the instruction manuals can save you embarrassment and ensure a smooth-running presentation.

Rehearse your presentation in advance! Review your visuals with your narration. Try to anticipate questions that might arise. You'll be rewarded for the time and effort you invest with greater self-confidence and poise. And your audience will experience a more effective presentation.

You may never have given a presentation before, but, with the help of good visuals and with conscientious rehearsal, you can begin to rank as a skilled presenter. Obviously, properly selected and presented visual aids can add significantly to the power and impact of your presentation. Remembering the six key P's—Proper Preparation and Practice Prevent Poor Performance—will help you achieve the results you want.

GROUP INVOLVEMENT

5

There's More To Teaching
Than Talking to Them

BASICS FOR GROUP INVOLVEMENT

Group involvement is scary to a lot of trainers—especially those with backgrounds strongly oriented toward lecture. One argument given is that time is too short to allow participation; there's too much content to cover. But the question is: "Is our job as instructors simply to cover the material —or to empower our participants to perform better back on the job?" I think it's to empower participants to perform better back on the job.

Consider the following statistics on retention. We retain:

> 10% of what we read,
> 20% of what we hear,
> 30% of what we see,
> 50% of what we hear and see,
> 70% of what we say, and
> 90% of what we say and do.

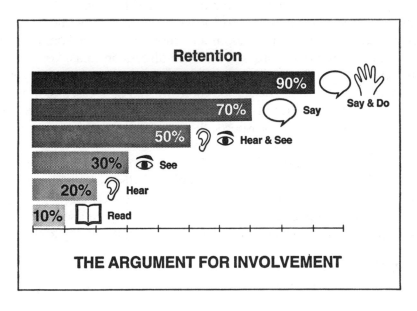

THE ARGUMENT FOR INVOLVEMENT

One of my "Laws of Adult Learning" is that "people don't argue with their own data." If I say something, I've got to believe it; after all, I'm teaching it. But if a participant says something, he or she will accept and believe it more fervently.

If we want people to apply what they've learned when they're back on the job, they've got to do two things: buy in to the concepts or skills we've introduced and retain them. Involvement is the key to both buy-in and retention.

Some trainers argue against involvement because they fear it reduces their control. To them, lecture appears to give them more control over their participants. My experience is different. Properly used, participation requires much less effort on the part of the instructor because the learners can manage and control themselves—and they will, given the proper structure and opportunity.

Over the years, I have learned to use an approach to group involvement that I call "instructor-led, participant-centered." It focuses as many of the learning activities as possible on the participants themselves. Sure, it requires some thought and creativity, but it can be a powerful learning tool that produces positive results.

In order to use the approach successfully, you, the trainer, must answer a couple of questions about your participants.

1. What experience/knowledge do they bring to the class? If they have none, you'll need some background information before you can expect much participation.

I once got a call from an instructor who said, "My class is bombing! I tried involvement, but it isn't working." I asked for details. He had carefully structured an opening discussion for his class of new salespeople. He distributed the discussion questions and chose a member from each small group to read the questions and lead the discussion. Alas, very little discussion followed. The problem lay in his first question: How do you find prospective customers? The reason there was so little discussion was because the class consisted of new salespeople with no experience. If they had known how to find prospects, they probably wouldn't have been in the class.

The solution was equally clear: The participants needed some information before they could have a meaningful discussion. The instructor then prepared a reference card describing seven different prospecting methods and giving an example of how each could be used. Participants then could consider each method in terms of its applicability to their product, territory, etc.

2. What do the participants need to know when the class is over, and what will they need to be able to find?

For example, in a class on conflict management, we cover five ways to deal with an angry person. It's important that participants know those five steps. If someone walks into your office, slams a fist on the table, and yells, "I'm fed up, and I'm not going to take it anymore!," you won't help the situation by flipping through the conflict manual to "Step one—acknowledge the anger" and then saying, "You seem upset." You need to *know* that information—and know it cold.

Or, to use a more dramatic example, consider cardiopulmonary resuscitation (CPR). When you need to apply it, both hands, your mouth, and absolute concentration are imperative. You can't stop and look in a manual to learn the techniques.

The things people need to know and do almost without thinking are great candidates for participation and involvement. As a matter of fact, they almost demand it. These topics probably will take up the bulk of your training time because of their importance. The things your participants need to be able to find, such as material in a reference manual, can also utilize participation; the more familiar they are with the manual, the quicker they'll be able to find things back on the job.

One thing I've learned in training and presenting and almost every trainer or speaker quickly learns as he or she gets involved in a group is that people like to talk to one another. They like to socialize. These basic elements of human behavior can be used to create powerful learning experiences that will get results for our participants.

──────────────── **INSIDER'S TIP** ────────────────

When designing a presentation, remember CPR:

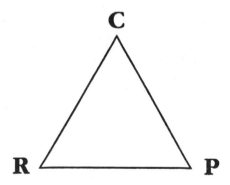

- Make sure the **C**ontent is relevant.
- Make sure you allow for adequate **P**articipation.
- Make sure you find ways to **R**eview and **R**einforce the key points.

If we're going to use group involvement effectively, we need to consider some simple guidelines.

1. The physical arrangement you use for training can communicate to participants that participation is expected and encouraged.

Your room arrangement helps determine instructor control, sight lines (how well can participants see each other, the instructor, visuals, etc.), and participation. Here are six common arrangements used in training.

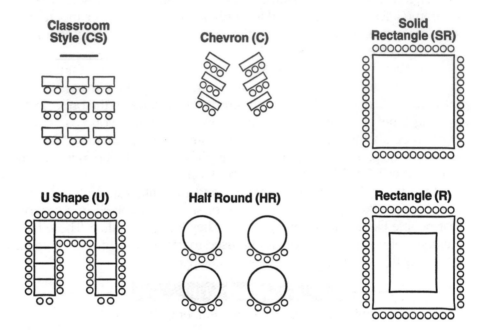

What do you want? High, medium, or low control as an instructor? High, medium, or low eye contact between participants? High, medium, or low participation from your attendees? The physical room arrangement can greatly influence these factors.

	CS	U	HR	C	R	SR
Control	H	H	M	M	M	M
Sightlines	L	M	H	H	M	M
Participation	L	M	H	H	L	M

2. Numerous techniques can be used to generate group involvement.

Some of them involve the entire group—be it 15, 20, 200, or 500 people—as a whole. For example, a lecture is a type of whole-group involvement. Of course, if only some people in the group are asking questions, they're more involved than others.

Another, more effective way to involve an entire group is to break that group down into smaller units. For example, you can get 200 people involved by breaking them up into pairs (dyads) or trios (triads).

If you're able to, you might seat people in half rounds or herringbone style as described earlier. When this is possible, I recommend seating people in rounds of five to seven each. Leave part of the table open, the part that faces you or is closest to where you'll be speaking and using visuals. That way, people can be involved with one another as you're structuring those opportunities, and, at the same time, they can easily see you as you're giving instructions or presenting various parts of the program.

I recommend small groups of five to seven for good reason. With more than seven people, some will tend to get lost in the group and not participate, particularly if they're shy. If you have fewer than five people, it becomes more possible for one person to dominate the group or the discussion.

3. Group leaders help stimulate group involvement.

If you break your larger group (for example, 50 participants) into smaller groups (for example, groups of five), group leaders can facilitate group activities in several ways.

A. The group leader leads the group through the activity according to directions given by the instructor. You may give directions verbally, or you may have them printed and handed out. If you hand out project sheets, you have two choices. You can give them only to the group leaders, who then read the assigned project, directions, or discussion questions aloud. Or you can provide each person with a discussion or activity or project sheet so the whole group can follow along as the project is covered.

B. The group leader reads aloud each project as the other participants at the table follow along. Although some group leaders may want participants to read on their own with a discussion to follow, this is less effective. When the leader reads aloud, participants benefit in four ways.

1. The group as a whole focuses on each individual issue.

2. By seeing and hearing at the same time, participants retain more. This may be very important for participants who are not particularly good readers.

3. The confidence of the group leader increases. The leader reads as the others listen and follow the leader's direction. This can further be reinforced by occasionally giving only the group leader the project.

4. It gives each participant a leadership role. If the activity is read by the group leader, the leader's role is clearly established. The role of group leader is rotated among the participants so that each person in the group has an opportunity.

C. The group leader can succinctly summarize the conclusions or discussion of the group. He or she simply stands, facing the other participants, and gives a brief report. Group leaders shouldn't deliver their reports while seated; being a group leader means acquiring basic presentation skills, such as addressing a group, in a variety of settings.

Each group leader's report should be brief. I usually allow only one minute, and I stick firmly to that limit for these reasons.

1. Anyone can talk for a minute. Allowing all group leaders the same short time minimizes comparisons in presentation styles —which isn't our primary focus.

2. It helps insure that each group leader will have something fresh to contribute—even those who report second or third.

3. It keeps the more verbal leaders from rambling. To end a group-leader report, use a simple phrase such as, "Okay, thank you very much." Natural pauses in the normal speaking pattern will allow you to terminate the report. I recommend that you don't comment on group-leader reports but conclude each one in the same congenial, neutral manner.

With groups larger than 25, not every group leader can report on every project. Generally, I will ask for three group-leader reports, and, when those are given, I'll occasionally ask if other leaders have anything else to add.

4. How you distribute materials depends upon the size of the group.

When 40 or more participants are going through the program simultaneously, you might put all program materials in a single binder, distributed at the beginning. If this is the case, you may not want to sequence all your material in chronological order because some participants tend to look ahead several pages to try to "psych" out the objectives. If you want people to discover and explore their own thoughts, you don't want to tip them off by having them read discussion materials intended for future use. This problem can be solved either by placing some pages further back in the manual, out of the regular sequence, or by holding some pages out of the manual, to be distributed at the appropriate time.

If you have large groups, you may want to precount your additional materials and have group leaders pick them up at the appropriate times, rather than distributing the materials to each group or to each participant yourself.

Whenever you use the instructor-led, participant-centered approach, you'll have to be aware of how much you allow your participants to rely on you. I generally try to clarify instructions if necessary, but I don't let myself be drawn into group discussions or debates—even if the group seems "stuck" or divided about which approach to take. Remember, the emphasis with this approach is on giving our participants experiences that will enable them to apply the content back on the job when their instructors aren't readily available to solve every problem or answer every question. The more we answer their questions and solve their problems in class and the more dependent they become, the less effective they'll be on the job. We want to provide a supportive environment for their exploration, struggle, and discovery so that the insights they gain will truly be theirs—as well as the self-confidence that comes from those discoveries.

THE INSTRUCTOR'S ROLE IN AN INSTRUCTOR-LED, PARTICIPANT-CENTERED TRAINING PROGRAM

If you're going to use the instructor-led, participant-centered approach, which generates maximum group involvement, you must position yourself carefully as the instructor. The more you or I take the role of the expert or the authority, the less likely people are to seek their own answers and to work through their own problems. They become more inclined to regard you as the final authority in terms of whether or not the discoveries reached in their group discussions were "correct." In the belief that the instructor should be more a facilitator or coordinator than an "expert," I offer the following explanation of this challenging role.

The Responsibility
It must be emphasized that the purpose of every training session is to assist the participants in developing their own answers, applying tools and techniques, using reference manuals, and tapping their own resources and those of their colleagues to reach solutions that work, both in class and on the job.

In situations where there are right and wrong answers, participants should be provided with resources and models that allow them to develop their own correct approaches and solutions. They must use what they know and have access to, rather than having the instructor either "come to the rescue" or play "judge" by determining right and wrong. Our purpose as trainers is not primarily to counsel, interpret, instruct, or in any other way lead people to believe that we are going to supply the answers to their questions. Instead, we should let the seminar, the instruments, the projects, the case studies, and other materials serve as resources that the participants can draw on to solve their problems and develop appropriate plans of action.

Life is a do-it-yourself project, just as our daily work activities are, for the most part, do-it-yourself projects. This instructional approach attempts, as much as possible, to mirror that. It's designed to allow participants to gain insight into how they learn, solve problems, find appropriate resources, etc., so they can be better equipped to meet their daily challenges. It can also, as a byproduct, help them develop better ways of relating to co-workers in order to be more productive on the job.

For your own benefit, then, and for that of your participants, it is important at the outset that you make it clear that you are there to lead and to guide but not to be the authority (even though your education and profession have made you one). Instructor-led, participant-centered training is designed to be a do-it-yourself project: the participants put the effort in and get a return on that effort for themselves. The insights, discoveries, and decisions they make must be theirs, not yours, for they will be responsible for implementing them after your time together.

This will take greater self-discipline on your part than any other method you might choose to use. But by exercising that discipline, you will help your participants gain self-discovery that cannot be obtained in any other way. Your role may not seem as significant as others you might take in instructing, but it is. Your visibility may not be as great, but your impact is greater.

I once had a participant in a seminar who had moved his family to a farm in order to provide a more wholesome environment for raising children. One day, he and one of his young daughters were watching some ducklings hatch from eggs. As one was struggling to break from its shell, the little girl tried to help by cracking the shell and setting the duckling free. An hour later, the duckling was dead. Said her father, "From that experience, we learned that the struggle to break from the shell was part of the process that equipped the duckling with the survival skills to live life. Without going through that process, it couldn't survive."

The lesson they learned is analogous to what trainers soon learn in the classroom: let participants struggle to attain rewards. Your role may not seem significant, but it is. The approach I recommend limits lecture and maximizes discovery and participation. Sometimes, it may not seem as if you're needed, but you are—often in ways the participants don't perceive. Ideally, you're the best kind of teacher—a facilitator of insight, change, and growth who teaches that answers come from within. Your personal attitudes and your role modeling will set the tone for your participants. And your seriousness of purpose, your personal planning, and your adherence to the guidelines you establish, along with your interest and enthusiasm for both the content and the participants, will facilitate change and learning for each of your participants.

You may face some problems. Some participants may not cooperate. Or they may seem indifferent, be late for sessions, or make critical comments. But that's part of the process. If you're patient, the participants themselves will resolve these problems. It's part of the chemistry of small-group interaction. Small-group members are accountable for one another —sometimes without realizing it—and the behavior of one member reflects on the others. Each person, then, becomes part of the change process for every other person. And you're a part of that process, too. Change can be difficult, but it does happen.

Fortunately, most participants will be supportive and enthusiastic, but some will not. They will complain, criticize, rationalize, joke, or withdraw. Understand this and don't be thrown by it. Your patience and understanding in the face of this resistance will eventually produce a breakthrough. By being patient, understanding, and positive, you will empower your participants to achieve the objectives of the course. Your participants will react the way you react. By demonstrating confidence in the ultimate value of this approach and maintaining your subtle leadership role, you will encourage them to react positively.

Don't abandon your role as a leader. Maintain control in a low key way and stick to your schedule. Respect your participants by starting and ending on time. Show your interest by being available to talk with them for at least 15 minutes before and after each class, and make your planning and preparation evident. These steps will create a strong program. Stick to your outline as closely as possible. Other ideas and enhancements to the program undoubtedly will surface; save them to structure follow-up sessions, either planned or voluntary. If your participants want to continue meeting on some voluntary, self-controlled basis after completing the program, discuss this possibility with them after the program is over.

Group Management

Small-group dynamics begin with participants in a program forming groups of from five to seven people. Different activities or projects are then given to these groups to be discussed or completed within a specific time.

Adults generally need more physical movement than they are provided in most training programs. If your program consists of day-long blocks, try to rotate the groups twice a day. If, for example, you have five groups, this can be accomplished by having the participants number off one through five and then grouping all the ones together, all the twos together, and so on. This permits all participants to interact with people they may not know. If you have some people who are resistant, it also keeps any one group from having to deal with them for the entire program. In each rotation, you move away from everyone you've been with. If you've been with someone who's resistant and negative, you're now relieved of that challenge.

You can rotate groups about every three hours. The number of ways you can rotate is limited only by your imagination. Assuming you have five groups of five each, here are two of the simplest methods.

1. Number one through five around the room. Rotate so each person sits with the others having the same number. Five completely new groups are formed.

2. Have everyone stand and form groups of three people while standing. (There will be one group of four). Each person in the group must be from a different table. Ask each person to share one thing he or she has learned. Next, ask that they form groups of five; again, each person must be someone new to the others. The fives now share one idea they've learned from their group of three. After this, the fives now become a new group and join each other at a table.

Different individuals should serve as group leaders for each project. This can be an opportunity to inject a little fun and humor in the program. Here are some ways I've used to choose group leaders.

• Say, "I'd like one person from each table to volunteer to do something. Once you've volunteered, I'll tell you what you're going to do." Generally, this is greeted by some laughter. After you have one volunteer from each table say, "Great, you've just volunteered to help me find the first group leaders. They're the people seated to the left of every volunteer."

• I ask everyone to point a finger in the air, and then I say, "At the count of three, point to the person at your table who should be the leader." The person with the most fingers pointed at him or her leads.

• The leader is the person with the largest high school graduating class...

• Or the person with the smallest high school graduating class...

• Or the person with the most letters in his or her first name (or nickname)...

• Or with the fewest letters.

• When there are three minutes left in the break, I'll say, "Group leaders, you have three minutes to find the rest of your group and get them back on time. Your new group leader will be the person at your table who sits down last."

At the beginning of the unit, you might want to have each group number individually around their groups. Then appoint each "number one" to be his or her group's leader. Generally, after you've been going for a while, the group will simply rotate to be sure that the opportunity is shared. Try to shift the responsibility of group leader around as much as possible.

THE ACTIVITY/DISCUSSION/ APPLICATION APPROACH

The activity/discussion/application formula provides an effective way to structure group-involvement activities. That is, we first do an activity. Then we discuss what went on. How did the participants and observers feel during the activity, and what happened as a result? The final step is to consider application. In other words, how can this activity be applied back on the job? How does it apply to real-life situations?

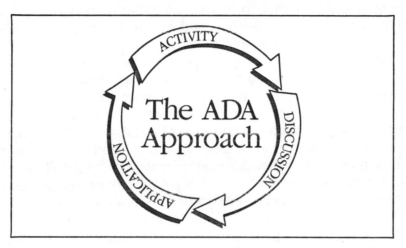

What I call the "potato activity" makes good use of the activity/discussion/application formula. Early in the seminar, I start giving people potatoes as rewards. If they make an interesting comment, I'll thank them and give them a potato. If they're helpful, I'll thank them and give them a potato. Sometimes, I'll simply give a potato at random. From time to time, I'll ask the "keepers of the potatoes" to pass their potato to someone else at another table. Needless to say, this peculiar potato business piques participant curiosity.

Then, just before a program break, I say, "I'd like those of you who have a potato to take it with you during the break and give it to someone who has not had a potato today. And if you receive a potato, you can give it to someone else who has not received a potato today." During the break, six or eight potatoes are passed around like crazy, as participants discuss with each other the point of this potato caper.

After the break, I generally lecture for a few minutes and then I ask the people who have the potatoes to stand, and I tell them one last time to pass the potatoes to someone at another table. I then ask the people who now have potatoes to come up front, and I give each of them a soda straw.

I say to the group, "One of the things we've talked about is that the key to motivation is belief. So let me ask how many of you believe I can tell these people how to drive their straws through their potatoes with a single blow. Notice, I said *tell*. I won't demonstrate this, so they won't actually see it done. I'll simply tell them how to do it, and then they'll do it.

How many of you believe that? Could I see a show of hands?" Generally, about a third of the hands will go up. Then I'll reach into my pocket and take out a $20, or a $50, or a $100 bill and say, "How many of you believe so much that you'd be willing to bet $20 or $50 or $100 that I can do it?" Generally, all the hands drop. So I say, "What we're really talking about is that the key to motivation is belief. And if we do believe, are we willing to put our money where our mouths are?"

Now, it's time to explain to the people standing up front how to put the straw through the potato. I begin by stressing that the secret here is following through. First, they must hold the straw in a closed fist with a thumb over the top and say "follow through" out loud together. In their other hand, they cup the potato so their hand forms a "C" around it. No one should hold the potato in the palm of their hand because they could hurt themselves when they drive the straw through. "After all," I say, "we wouldn't want any OSHA violations!" If you're working with business-people, trainers, or personnel people, you'll get a laugh at this because they're only too aware of complicated OSHA regulations.

I then tell them to practice a couple more times. Then, when they're ready, they can simply drive the straw through the potato. Once again, I remind them that the key is following through, not the amount of power that's used. "Simply draw your straw back when you're ready, and, as you bring it forward, say out loud, 'Follow through.'" Generally, over half the people will do it the first time; with a couple more tries and maybe new straws for those who break them, everybody will get it. I then have everyone give the participants a hand and suggest that they might want to take the potatoes back to their tables as souvenirs.

We're now ready to discuss what just occurred. This discussion can involve the entire group together, or you can break the group into small units for discussions. The purpose of the discussion is to consider the following questions. What was the difference between *showing* and *telling?* Did it matter whether or not the participants believed entirely that they could accomplish the activity at the beginning? How did a willingness to try affect their ability to participate and succeed?

Here are three other methods that can be used for making sure that content is well taught.

1. E-T-A—Experience Theory Awareness
We first provide people with an experience; we then give them the theory behind what happened or why the experience worked the way it did, and that leads to awareness.

For example, people come into a training room that has half-round tables rather than a traditional school-room style. They begin interacting with one another and later we start to explore the differences between room arrangements. When you're seated at a half-round with five to seven people, you instantly form a group and that begins to develop a sense of accountability to the group both in terms of involvement and participation and behavior. Our behavior now reflects on our group. Having discussed this theory, people then become aware that half-rounds may be much more useful for teaching than the traditional school-room style.

2. E-A-T—Experience Awareness Theory

Sometimes we'll provide people with an experience and they won't even need the theory. In the very process in going through the experience, they get an "A-HA!" The theory merely gives them a reason for why it worked, though intuitively they now know it works because they've experienced it.

In a seminar, after presenting information in a variety of ways for about an hour and a half, you stop and have participants make an "Action Idea" list. They begin to list the ideas that they've picked up that they can use back on the job. Once they've had a couple of minutes to do this, you now have them share with their table their Action Ideas. As they listen to others at their table, other Action Ideas they're hearing may appeal to them, and they can add them to their own list.

Then, you have each table share an Action Idea with the other participants in the room, and you go from table to table until a master list of all the Action Ideas is formed. Again, at this point, if anyone hears an idea that appeals to them they can add it to their Action Idea list. As you go through this process, there may be people that say to themselves, "Gee, this is a really good process! It's good to stop and take time to list these Action Ideas. I'm going to use that in my next class." Later you talk about the importance of reflection time—the importance of taking time occasionally to stop and give people a chance to reflect here and now on what they're learning rather than simply continuing to dump content and never allowing any time to reflect.

You could also emphasize the importance of reviewing without calling it review. In allowing a reflection time, people are basically reviewing their own content. In allowing people to share their Action Ideas in a small group setting, there is review and reinforcement going on. Some of it is reinforcement, because people are hearing others talk about the same Action Ideas they have listed. Review is going on because they may hear ideas that hadn't occurred to them because their focus was someplace else as that particular idea was being demonstrated in the classroom. The theory that you've discussed about the importance of reflection and review simply reinforces the awareness that they gain because they realized that, in the Action Idea process, they liked the idea and were going to use it. They had an experience that created awareness—this theory simply reinforced it.

3. *T-E-A—Theory Experience Awareness*

Sometimes participants may have no information or experience on the subject at all, so we need to present some theory first, then we can give them an experience that then leads to awareness.

If you were teaching a sales training program, it might be important to discuss the theory of closing—what needs to be done before asking for the order, and the basic steps in closing which might also include handling objections and put-offs. Then you can provide people with the experience of actually using the tested closing pattern or handling the most common objections using answers that have been worked out through experience. That then leads them to an awareness that having a method and a planned way for closing and dealing with objections is much more powerful than "winging it" or simply hoping that people will buy.

THINGS TO REMEMBER ABOUT INSTRUCTOR-LED, PARTICIPANT-CENTERED TRAINING

1. Start on time; end on time. If you wait for stragglers before you begin, each session will start a little later, and you will, in effect, be teaching them to be late. If the members know you start precisely on schedule, they will learn to be prompt. I always try to start with some value-added material that is useful but not critical. That way, I can start on time and reward those who are punctual but not have those who are late miss vital information.

2. Not every project has to be completed. If I introduce an activity where sequence is not critical, I can have each group start on different parts of the activity. During the reporting process, all the participants become familiar with all the information. This method keeps everything moving along briskly. If the participants are always wishing they had a little more time, you will retain their appetites for the program.

3. Try to maintain your role as a facilitator. Do not preach, lecture, or inject your own thinking. Do not top off discussions and reports with your own opinions. Obviously, you're familiar with the content of the program and could, therefore, give summaries filled with dazzling insight. But that's not the purpose. People value their own discoveries. If they feel they're competing with you, they'll give up and take an "Okay, wise guy, you tell us" stance that will kill any participation.

4. Avoid the "boss" image. Lead by example. If you criticize, embarrass, or make jokes about participants, you'll lose the respect of the group. If people express differing viewpoints, value them even if you don't agree with them.

5. Learn the names of your participants. Be available to everyone.

6. Encourage the participants to mix. Change the groups frequently to build a cohesive spirit among your entire class and to discourage the formation of cliques.

7. Make individuals' problems the group's problems. If an individual asks you a question, respond by saying, "That's an interesting question. Do you mind if I ask the other members for their impressions?" You should become an example of correct attitude rather than an authority. By turning individual questions into class projects, you help participants grow.

8. Don't engage in "debate" with participants about who is right or wrong. Instead, help them use the resources that are available to find the right answers in those cases where there is a right and wrong.

9. Help each participant work with all the other participants. We can't always choose the people we work with or for. Understanding and growth can be fostered by focusing the small groups on common problems and helping them use their combined resources to find solutions.

10. Be the first one there and the last one to leave. Check out the facilities. Arrange your material so you are fully prepared to conduct the session.

11. Personify the spirit of the program. That is, be enthusiastic, cheerful, positive, considerate.

12. Use a casual leadership style. Avoid abrupt commands such as "Stop!" Comments such as "Let's get started" or "The time is up" indicate a more relaxed approach. Remember, the participants are adults who like to be in control, so try to suggest rather than order.

13. Avoid eavesdropping or sitting in on discussions.

14. Maintain the time limit on group-leader reports. Be gentle but firm on this point. Not maintaining this control is the cause of most participant complaints.

INSIDER'S TIP

Music can be useful as a group involvement aid.
- Bright, uplifting music as people come in can set the tone.
- Reflective music can help as people work on an individual basis.
- Moderately paced music can help keep small group discussions moving, and help mask nearby conversation.
- Game show style music can add a new dimension to games and simulations.
- Either raising or lowering music volume can serve to indicate the wrap-up of any time period.

METHODS OF INSTRUCTION

A method of instruction is a system by which information is presented or sought for the purpose of solving problems, gaining new understandings, developing or experiencing new attitudes.

There are numerous ways to present content; here are some of the most common.

Method: Lecture
Description: One person systematically presenting information
Advantages: Presents maximum information in a limited time. Makes it possible to arrange diverse materials and ideas in an orderly system of thought.
Limitations: Uses one person's point of view, one channel of communication, and no group participation. Is strongly influenced by the personality of the speaker.
Pattern of Interaction:

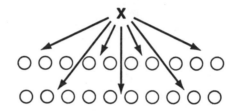

Method: Question and Answer
Description: One person provoking response by inquiry, usually from person to person
Advantages: Provides for clarification of information to answer specific needs of learner. Easily combined with other methods.
Limitations: Tends to become too formal, threatening, and embarrassing; group may become bored and lose interest.
Pattern of Interaction:

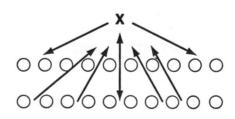

Method: Group Discussion

Description: Two or more persons sharing knowledge, experiences, and opinions, building on ideas, clarifying, evaluating, and coordinating to reach an agreement or gain better understanding

Advantages: Meets the needs of group members by providing high degree of interaction, interest, and involvement.

Limitations: Does not provide authoritative information nor is it helpful for large groups. Requires time, patience, and capable leadership.

Pattern of Interaction:

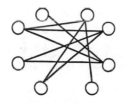

Method: Lecture Forum

Description: One person combining the lecture with asking questions for clarification of specific points

Advantages: Combines with the lecture a two-way communication for clarification of ideas and meeting specific needs.

Limitations: Presents one person's viewpoint in answering questions that will tend to be perfunctory and limited to a few persons.

Pattern of Interaction:

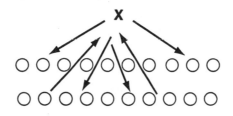

Method: Symposium

Description: Three or more persons with different points of view present-ing short speeches followed by questions and answers under the direction of a moderator

Advantages: Presents several viewpoints and, through questions, clarifies information to meet specific needs.

Limitations: Requires speakers with equal ability, a skillful chairperson, and freedom of participation.

Pattern of Interaction:

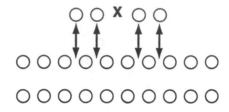

Method: Panel

Description: Three or more persons discussing an issue before a group under the direction of a moderator, followed by a group discussion

Advantages: Presents different viewpoints to stimulate thinking.

Limitations: Needs skillful moderator to keep panel on subject and to keep a limited number of questioners from monopolizing the discussion. Needs a balanced panel to keep personalities from influencing opinions.

Pattern of Interaction:

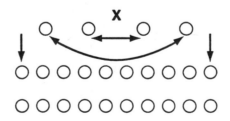

Method: Debate

Description: Two speakers, under the direction of a moderator, presenting two sides of an issue

Advantages: Sharpens the issue for a group by presenting both sides. Holds interest and clarifies questions.

Limitations: Tends to become emotional, requiring a good moderator to mediate differences.

Pattern of Interaction:

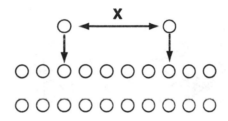

Method: Conversations

Description: Two people informally discussing a topic before an audience

Advantages: Provides information in an informal setting, adding interest and emotional appeal as it encourages discussion.

Limitations: Needs careful planning to keep from becoming disorganized or dominated by personality of participants.

Pattern of Interaction:

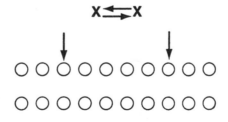

Method: Buzz Groups
Description: A large group divided into smaller groups of 5-10 discussing a particular topic and then reporting back to the larger group
Advantages: Promotes enthusiasm and involvement as it provides opportunity for maximum discussion in limited time.
Limitations: Discussion tends to be shallow, disorganized, and easily dominated by one or two in the group. Needs skillful leader to handle the process.
Pattern of Interaction:

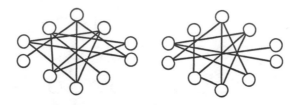

Method: Role-Playing
Description: Selected members of a group spontaneously acting out a human relations situation or incident, followed by analysis and evaluation
Advantages: Provides opportunity to "feel" human relations situations and experiment with possible solutions.
Limitations: Tends to be artificial and merely entertaining unless carefully handled. May become an end in itself unrelated to group problem.
Pattern of Interaction:

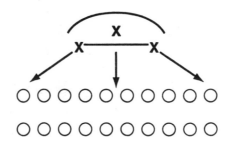

Method: Demonstrations

Description: One person illustrating a process before a group

Advantages: Illustrates techniques and skills and shows the results of particular procedures.

Limitations: Provides limited participation by group members.

Pattern of Interaction:

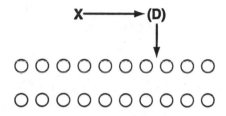

Method: Laboratory

Description: One or more persons solving problems through testing and experimentation

Advantages: Translates theory into practice, providing actual experience and first-hand information. Appeals to many senses and shows results by doing.

Limitations: Generally requires more time, special skills, and equipment.

Pattern of Interaction:

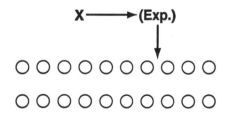

Method: Exhibits
Description: Showing an arrangement or collection of materials
Advantages: Displays needed information in visible form.
Limitations: Uses visual appeal only, lacking communication and discussion. Requires time and preparation.
Pattern of Interaction:

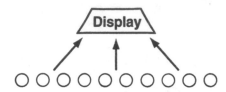

Method: Projects
Description: Group members cooperatively investigating a problem
Advantages: Offers first-hand information, stimulates interests, allows pursuit of personal interest, provides practical experience, and builds group closeness.
Limitations: Requires time for completion. Activity tends to become an end in itself.
Pattern of Interaction:

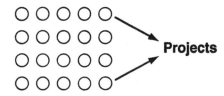

WAYS TO GET PARTICIPANTS BACK FROM BREAKS

Time
Use odd times, like "We'll break until 11:06."

Music
Play music during breaks and either significantly raise or lower the volume to signify the end of the break.

Rewards
Offer points for activities you want people involved in. For example – one point for each person who's back on time. Double point value if your whole table is back on time.

Town Crier
Appoint someone whose job it is to ring a school bell and announce the end of break. A participant can do this much more forcefully than an instructor.

Lights
Blink the lights on and off as they do in the theatre to signal five minutes until the curtain goes up.

Trivia
Offer a trivia question, word puzzle, or some other activity right near the end of the break to get people seated, reconnected, and reinvolved.

Tips
Often a quick training tip or two right as break ends. If someone chooses to be late they've missed a great tip or two.

Group Leader
Have each table go on break with a group leader responsible for on-time return. The group leader could be the first person to stand as the group starts the break—or the last person to stand, etc.

- Time

- Music

- Rewards

- Town Crier

- Lights

- Trivia

- Tips

- Group Leader

100

CREATIVE
MATERIALS 6

Projects, Case Studies and Role Plays That Encourage Students to Learn from Each Other and Their Shared Life Experiences

"Experience keeps a dear school," said Benjamin Franklin. "A fool can learn in no other." Experience requires that we pay the price of learning ourselves. But we have a choice; we can choose to learn from others who already have paid that price. We can learn vicariously from their experiences and thus accelerate our own learning experiences.

This chapter is about creating situations where participants can learn from their own experiences, as well as from experiences that you, the instructor, can provide. Sometimes, you'll want to create the situations in advance. Other times, it makes sense to have the participants go through the process of creating their own, using their own experiences and information. Whichever direction you choose (and you may choose both in the same program), you'll follow the same basic model.

MODEL FOR STRUCTURING PROJECTS

In structuring any kind of project, case study, or role play, you must consider seven steps.

Step 1. Select the Issue
What *issue* do you want to focus on? Is it managing conflict, resolving conflict, solving problems, or showing appreciation?

Step 2. Select the Incident/Situation
How are you going to approach the issue you've selected? If, for example, you're dealing with how emotions affect communications, you might choose an incident or situation involving a boss and a subordinate.

Step 3. Provide Enough Details to Enable Participants to Reach Decisions
For example, the role play described on pages 103 and 104 takes place between a department head and a supervisor. There's sufficient detail to conduct the role play and set the agenda and objectives.

Step 4. Tell Specifically What Kind of Product You Want

Do you want the group to answer a series of questions and be prepared to deliver a summary? Are participants supposed to devise an action plan that ought to be followed to resolve the situation? Make clear what you expect to get back from your participants when the project is over.

Step 5. Set the Group Size

Are people going to pair off? Are they going to work as a group on a project, case study, or role play? Will they do the task individually? Each of these options affects the dynamics of the activity.

Step 6. Set Your Mix

In other words, are you going to have men working together, women working together, managers working together, subordinates working together? Are you going to mix these kinds of groups? Are you going to have outside and inside salespeople separate or together? Take the time to think about the participants in the group. Is there value to rearranging them in specific ways to take advantage of the unique background or experience that certain members may have? Or perhaps random assignments will work just as well? In either case, think it through before you decide.

Step 7. Set Your Time Limits

How much time are you going to allow? In some projects we structure, we develop more material than any group can cover. This keeps everyone fully occupied during the time available. The most important discussion questions are at the beginning and the end. Assuming there are eight questions to discuss and 20 minutes available for discussion, after 15 minutes we'd ask the groups to move to question six, if they're not already there. This way, each group gets to the key material.

THE ROLE PLAY

You can ask people to approach a role-play situation in one of three ways.

1. Approach the role play exactly the way you would a real-life situation. In other words, you *are* this person, so handle the situation the way you would if you really were confronting it.

2. Approach it exactly as it's written in the project. Forget the fact that you don't agree with certain opinions, biases, etc., in the written project; just "follow the script," as it were.

3. Do it ideally. In other words, seize the opportunity to say and do things in the role play that you would never say or do in a real-life situation.

In this role-playing exercise, one participant will play the role of a department head. Tell that person: "Be forceful in presenting your argument; remember, you believe you're right."

You're the head of a 75-person department in a large organization. You are proud of the fact that you started out as an office clerk 20 years ago and that, by working hard and taking advantage of on-the-job training opportunities and a few night courses, you're the only high-school graduate in your organization to have a similar position.

In spite of your experience and expertise, however, one of your six supervisors is constantly bucking you. This person has been in the organization about a year and has received several promotions, largely on the strength of a recently earned master's degree. Particularly annoying is the way he interrupts department meetings with suggestions that are ill-timed and that throw your schedule out of kilter.

You believe that meetings should start and end on time, so you've called a private conference to discuss the matter. You feel the best solution is to meet privately before department meetings to review suggestions and select those that should be discussed in the general meeting. You know you need to make your points quickly and with no interruptions. You resent being interrupted and sidetracked from the issue at hand, and you expect others will respect your solution.

The other participant in this role-playing exercise will play the supervisor. Tell this person: "Be forceful in presenting your argument; remember, you believe you're right."

You are a supervisor responsible for 15 people in your organization. You have achieved this position in a little over a year, more because of your master's degree than your work experience. Others in your department look to you as an innovator. Your fellow supervisors seem to think you're headed for bigger and better things.

The one stumbling block seems to be your boss, the head of your department, who is responsible for 75 people including yourself and five other supervisors. The boss seems to be irritated with the perfectly valid suggestions you bring up in your department meetings. You get the feeling that the boss is threatened by your master's degree, perhaps because he himself didn't finish college. You also feel there may be some jealousy because you keep coming up with these great suggestions. You're scheduled for a personnel interview. You want to make sure you get full credit for your ideas; that's why you bring them up in front of everyone. Whatever your boss says, you want to be sure to clear the way for a time at each department meeting to suggest new ideas. Scheduling a specific time, say 10 or 15 minutes, would give you a forum for your thoughts and, at the same time, would appease your boss, who constantly harps about the importance of starting and ending on time.

You'll notice that a number of factors were considered in this role play between the department head and the supervisor.

- Each role is structured so the players have specific opinions.
- Each person enters the role play with a specific agenda.
- The role play can be used for several purposes.

1. People tend to get emotional in this role play so we can observe how they listen to one another's points of view.

2. Observers can focus on what happens when people enter a meeting with their minds already made up about the outcome.

3. We can discuss how to unblock emotions in certain situations.

4. We can consider alternative approaches to solving this problem. Sometimes, we encounter difficulty solving problems because we approach them with preconceived solutions. We're then blocked by these preconceptions from looking at other possible solutions.

Written Role Plays

Group involvement also can be generated by introducing an individual activity followed by a group activity. The following two projects illustrate this approach. The first, titled "Living Up to Your Potential," was given to participants to do individually in seven or eight minutes. Without sharing what they had written, they were asked to do the second project, "Achieving Your Expectations," as a group with a leader reporting their conclusions afterwards. Approximately 20 minutes were allowed for discussion.

You'll notice that we started with a project that individuals completed on their own. Then, in the group project, individuals worked together—exploring their feelings and expectations and realizing how these related to goal setting and other issues.

At the end of the individual activity—"Living Up to Your Potential"—no report was required to the larger group. But at the end of the "Achieving Your Expectations" activity, three or four group leaders summarized their discussions to all the groups in the seminar.

Ask participants to do one of the following exercises.

LIVING UP TO YOUR POTENTIAL

1. You are given access to your personnel file. In it is a glowing letter of recommendation about you written by your boss. It is the most gratifying letter you can imagine receiving.

Write in the space below what you would want the letter to say.

2. You are in your hometown. An old friend of yours and your spouse is having lunch with you. The friend asks, "Do you have any idea how much you are loved?" and hands you a letter. Your spouse wrote it, extolling your virtues, and gave it to your friend.

Write what you would like the letter to say in the space below.

After participants have completed writing their letters, ask the following questions to stimulate discussion.

1. What are your feelings about the letter you have just written? How would you feel if such a letter were written about you? How would it affect your expectations for yourself? How would it affect your relationship with the person who wrote it?

2. In writing that letter, you were, in a way, writing out your own ideal expectations for your life, painting a picture of the person you would like to be. What could you do to move closer to this ideal?

3. We hear a lot about the expectations of others and their effect on our ability to perform, but how about our own expectations? How do they affect how we perform?

4. Do you have expectations of the kind of person you would like to be and of what you would like to achieve? What are they?

5. What would it take to achieve these expectations?

6. How do experiences relate to goals and goal setting? How could goal setting help you realize your expectations?

7. How could affirmations help you to realize your expectations? What are some affirmations you could put to use in achieving your expectations?

When Role Reversal Can Make a Point

Role reversal is a concept that applies not only to role plays but also to other kinds of projects. Sometimes it helps us put ourselves in another person's shoes. This can be accomplished very effectively and can best be illustrated by this example of an activity that I use in a seminar about persuasion.

Very simply, what I do is have everyone in the group become either the editor of a union newsletter or the editor of a company newsletter. Then I announce to the group that the president of their company is about to come in and read the following prepared statement. Assuming the role of the president, I deliver this announcement.

"As you all know, the economy has hit our company particularly hard. Taking into consideration the substantial capital equipment purchases we have made in the past 12 months and the fact that we are able to operate at only 60 percent capacity due to significantly decreased sales, I must request that all employees agree to a 10 percent pay decrease and a freeze on raises for the next six months.

"Agreeing to this proposal should help insure that any necessary layoffs will be minimal. I would also hope that we would not have to extend our annual plant closing beyond the usual two weeks. Senior management of your company has already agreed unanimously to accept a 10 percent cut in their salaries.

"I regret having to make this request, but I feel it is in the best interests of the company and—in the long run—in your futures.

"Please sign the attached card stating your agreement and return it to the personnel office immediately."

After I read this statement, I ask the "editors" to write a four- or five-paragraph article from the viewpoint of their newsletter on this announcement. People can work on this individually, or they can work in groups. The union-newsletter groups, maybe at two or three tables, work together, and the company-newsletter group works at a separate table. When they're finished, several of the groups will read aloud their news articles, which obviously express certain biases.

As a final step, I ask the groups to reverse roles: those who were editors of the company newsletter are now editors of the union newsletter and vice versa. This produces a slingshot effect. Sometimes the groups are able to reverse roles very well; at other times, they're not. Either way, the point is made. If role reversal is difficult, the discussion centers around why. Frequently, the groups have become so biased that they can't switch positions. This situation stimulates discussion about the importance of keeping an open mind toward issues in order to solve problems and resolve conflict.

QUICK TIPS FOR ROLE-PLAY

- Role play in smaller groups of three to six. This minimizes the discomfort of "everyone's watching."
- Add a coach to the role play. The coach stands behind the person and either the coach or the role player can call a "time out" to talk about what to do or say next.
- Make the coach a "tag team" member. If the role player gets tuck, the coach can be "tagged" to switch places with the role player.

DESIGNING EFFECTIVE PROJECTS
AND CASE STUDIES

There are a number of strategies that can be used to make projects and case studies more effective. I'll use two projects that I developed for some of my programs to illustrate.

1. Janice Bell is the office manager of a small office with the responsibility of overseeing five clerks and typists. The job started small and has grown to where she is crowded for space. She's been on the job 20 years and this is the only job that she's ever had. Janice was fresh out of business school when she joined the firm. She likes the company and the people she works with. One day her boss asks for a private conference and says, "You and your people have been doing a wonderful job, but the load seems to be getting more than your people can handle. I've been giving it some thought and have checked around pretty carefully. I think the solution would be to get some computers and begin to use word processing. They have a special two week school that you and one of your people could go to that would teach you everything you need to know. What do you think?" Janice responds rather touchily, "My people work hard. The workload is growing, but we've solved that problem in the past by adding an extra person." Her boss feels word processing would be a better idea. Janice finally says that she'll send two people from her department, but she will not go herself.

Why do you think Janice was so touchy? Why would she turn down the opportunity for this training? What could her boss have said to make the situation more acceptable?

2. For the past six years your family has gone to the same lakeside cottage for your two week vacation. This year you feel it's time for a change. You've secretly put aside a little money each payday and a month before the vacation you say at dinner, "Surprise! I've been saving all year and this year our vacation's going to be special. We'll not only have the lakes, but also the mountains and the ocean." You pull out a fabulous full color brochure and describe the fantastic resort spots that your family can choose from this year, rather than the "same old, same old." To your dismay the plan is greeted rather unenthusiastically. No one seems to want to make a decision. Finally someone suggests that you just go back up to the lake and use the extra money to buy a new color TV. Now it's your turn to feel upset and dismayed. All your sacrifice – and it's not even appreciated.

Why do you think the family's acting this way? Is their resistance to a different vacation spot – or perhaps the fact that you didn't let them in on the planning? What could you have done to smooth the way for a favorable decision and enjoyable vacation?

1. Offer participants a choice. Rather than simply one case study, I offered two. You'll notice the first is business oriented, the second more personal. In some settings I might want to use one, or ther other—or both. Designing more than one provides me with flexibility—and my participants with a choice.

2. Be careful of your language. In the case of Janice Bell, if you read the material, you cannot tell whether Janice's boss is male or female. Don't make roles gender specific unless you absolutely have to. In the family vacation incident, I've asked people how many thought the person saving the money was male? Female? Then I point out that the case says *you* have been saving money. Many times people miss that. Men raise their hands saying they saw the person as female and vice versa.

3. Develop discussion materials that help debrief the activity.

Group Leader: Read aloud and discuss.

1. You have been discussing a difficult subject for people to grasp—change. Do you feel that people are naturally resistant to change—or do they resist the manner in which change is presented? Share any personal experiences where you may have resisted the manner change was presented rather than the change itself.

2. Why do you feel people are resistant to change? Were the "good old days" really that good? Or is it that we realize that time is moving on and if the good old days were back so would our youth? What are some other things that might cause this resistance?

3. Many people have set habits for literally everything they do—which shoe is put on first in the morning, where their coffee cup is, etc. Change is difficult because it means changing habits. How could changing little habits—like the route you take each morning or getting up 15 minutes earlier or taking a walk around the block before breakfast make changing other things easier? Discuss some things that you could do to alter your routine and bring a little "change" into your life.

4. What are some things that you've heard people say that might indicate to you that they are resisting change? (For example, have you heard, "But we've always done it that way"?)

5. Seeing the bigger picture can help you prepare for change. Where do you think the railroad would be today if they had seen themselves 50 years ago in the "transportation industry" rather than railroading? How about the motion picture industry if it had seen itself in the "entertainment industry"? What other illustrations can you think of where people and industries were bypassed because they refused to change when they had the opportunity?

6. What are some habits that you have that you would not want to change? Why not? What are some habits that you might want to develop?

7. How does your attitude affect the benefits that you get from change? Are there some changes that you have made (or been forced to make) in your life that you could see no benefits in at the time? What possible benefits can you see looking back? Can bigger benefits be derived from change by expecting positive results and benefits beforehand? Why?

In this example, after people have discussed the mini-cases, they debrief with a series of questions designed to help them look at the issue behind the cases—the challenge of change. Notice the questions begin with general questions (e.g., Why do you think people are resistant to change?) and end with more specific application questions (e.g., What are some habits that you would want to change?).

4. Develop value-added questions. In most classes you'll have two groups of people—the quick and the analytical. Developing value-added questions can help the analytical have the discussion time they need without the quick feeling as if they've wasted their time. Let's say you have seven discussion questions. The important questions are Questions 1, 2, 3, and 7. The value-added questions are 5 and 6. Once you see that an analytical group is on Question 4 you can say, "If you're not already there, please drop down to Question 7 and spend your last two minutes on it." In all likelihood the quick can't get through all seven before the analyticals get through their four.

5. Use the power of choice to overcome inertia. For example, let's say there are seven problems to solve. I'll say to people, "You have a choice. Start with 1 and work to 7 or or start with 7 and work to 1." People will usually look at both 1 and 7, choose the easiest and start there. The model is this: Questions 1 and 7 are the easiest, 2 and 6 next easiest, 3 and 5 more difficult, and 4 almost impossible. No one gets through all of them. When I debrief, someone gives a solution for 1, then someone 7, and so on. For half the group, they're checking the solution. For the other half, it's new because it's a problem they didn't work. It's another strategy that creates energy and interest.

THE GRID CONCEPT

This exercise works particularly well with groups of people who have some knowledge about or experience in the area you're exploring. One of the benefits of the grid concept is that it can be customized to the particular group you're working with.

The first example I offer here relates to training. The participants—say, 40 trainers or so in groups of five or six—brainstorm at their tables about the qualities and characteristics necessary for a person to be an effective trainer and/or speaker. Then I ask the groups, one at a time, to give me one characteristic from their list. Group 1 gives an item, Group 2 an item, and so on, until every group has named all its items, which I write down. While the participants are involved in the next project, I take the groups' suggestions and make them into an effectiveness grid.

Here are the results of one such effectiveness grid that was developed for the Central Wisconsin Chapter of American Society for Training and Development.

CENTRAL WISCONSIN ASTD'S
TRAINING EFFECTIVENESS GRID

	10	20	30	40	50	60	70	80	90	100
Communication Skills (Good)						X				
Enthusiastic							⊗			
Nice (Friendly)						X				
Tests (Evaluates)			X							
Ready (Prepared)					X					
Adaptable (Flexible)			⊗							
Listener						X				
Wisdom			⊗							
Innovative				X						
Sales Ability (Persuasive)						X				
Conscientious							⊗			
Organized					X					
Neat (Well-dressed)						X				
Sensitive			X							
Interest in Others						X				
Natural Warmth				X						
Assortment (Variety)		⊗								
Sees People (Eye contact)				X						
Tolerant (Patient)				X						
Dedicated								⊗		

Three Greatest Strengths
1. _Enthusiastic_
2. _Conscientious_
3. _Dedicated_

Three Greatest Needs
1. _Adaptable_
2. _Wisdom_
3. _Assortment_

Each trainer got a copy of this grid and then did a self-rating on how effective he or she was in each of the areas listed. They circled the three they saw as their greatest strengths and the three they saw as their greatest needs on the grid and then, at the bottom of the grid, they could list their three strongest and three weakest areas. They did not necessarily rate their three weakest areas, those that needed improvement, as the lowest because they may not have had to use those skills in their particular function as trainers.

I concluded this exercise by saying, "The qualities and characteristics listed on your grid are those mentioned when people are asked, 'What do you need to be a successful trainer?' Actually, most of these qualities could be applied not just to being successful as a trainer but to being successful in general.

"One of the most important things to notice about the grid is that every one of us can acquire and manage each of the qualities and characteristics listed. Even energy, for example, can be managed. It's been discovered that we burn three times as much energy when we think negatively as when we think positively and are in control of our emotions and actions.

"By way of illustration, imagine for a moment that you're all single. For those of you who are, that's easy. But the rest of you imagine it as well. Now, you're all single, and you've had a lousy day. No one loves you, and the day just seems to drag on and on. Every time you look at your watch, it seems as though it's going backwards.

"Finally, this lousy day ends. You slump into you car, drive home, walk through the door, collapse on the couch. You don't even have enough energy to turn on the boob tube.

"As you're lying there in a stupor, the phone rings. You answer it, and it happens to be someone of the opposite sex whom you've admired—hopelessly, you thought—from afar. 'I know it's really short notice,' says this person, 'but I happen to have a couple of tickets for [an event you've been dying to go to]. I wonder if you'd like to go with me tonight?' And you say, 'Well, I really appreciate the offer, but it's been such a lousy day. I think I really just want to take a nice hot bath and go to bed.' Right? Wrong!

"In that situation, each of us would suddenly have all the energy we need to go out and enjoy that evening's activity, because something crucial has just changed. And it's changed pretty dramatically. What is it?"

When people answer "attitude," they're absolutely right. Remember, we burn three times as much energy when thinking negatively as when we're thinking positively and are in control of our emotions and actions. All the things we've discussed here can be acquired, developed, and managed by each of us. The area on the left-hand side of the line we made on the Central Wisconsin ASTD grid represents what we are right now. The area on the right-hand side represents our potential, what we can be. The entire focus of our training should be to help those we train acquire, develop, and manage the skills and characteristics needed to be effective.

This concept can be used for other topics as well. It could, for instance, be a problem-solving or decision-making or sales-effectiveness grid. In the example that follows, it happens to deal with customer courtesy.

CAESARS BOARDWALK REGENCY'S CUSTOMER SERVICE/COURTESY EFFECTIVENESS GRID

	10	20	30	40	50	60	70	80	90	100
Courteous										
Appearance (Good)										
Eye Contact										
Smiles										
Acts to Solve Problems										
Responsive										
Self-Image (Positive)										
Be-of-Service Attitude										
Organized										
Amiable (Friendly)										
Reliable (Follows through)										
Detail-oriented										
Withholds Judgment										
Attitude (Positive)										
Listens										
Knowledge of Job & Hotel/Casino										
Remembers Names										
Empathy (Understanding)										
Genuinely Helpful										
Energetic (Motivated)										
Needs to be Responsible										
Communicates Clearly										
Yourself										

This grid was designed for Caesars Boardwalk Regency, a hotel/casino in Atlantic City. It's based upon interviews my partner and I conducted; we asked people what they looked for when they went to a hotel or casino or restaurant. What were the hallmarks, from the customer's perspective, of real courtesy? We took the 85 characteristics from the interviews and boiled them down into the qualities represented on the Caesars Boardwalk Regency acrostic. This became the company's customer-courtesy effectiveness grid, and it formed the basis for a training program on customer service and courtesy for all 3500 employees of Caesars Boardwalk Regency.

This third example is a computer literacy grid that was designed for our Computer Literacy for Executives and Managers seminar. This grid was based on the actual course content to be covered. We wanted a self-rating at the beginning of the course to find out how much each manager already knew so that their expertise could be incorporated into the course as we proceeded.

COMPUTER LITERACY GRID

	10	20	40	60	80	100
Computer Software	___	___	___	___	___	___
Operating Skills	___	___	___	___	___	___
Memory (Storage)	___	___	___	___	___	___
Printers	___	___	___	___	___	___
Utilities	___	___	___	___	___	___
Terminology	___	___	___	___	___	___
Electronic Spread Sheet	___	___	___	___	___	___
Records (Data Bs. Mgmt.)	___	___	___	___	___	___
Lease/Purchase Decision	___	___	___	___	___	___
Information Services	___	___	___	___	___	___
Telepro (Comm.)	___	___	___	___	___	___
Elements (Concepts)	___	___	___	___	___	___
Remote (Distributed)	___	___	___	___	___	___
Applications	___	___	___	___	___	___
Components (Hardware)	___	___	___	___	___	___
You & Change	___	___	___	___	___	___
Graphics	___	___	___	___	___	___
Requirements (Needs)	___	___	___	___	___	___
Info Processing (Word)	___	___	___	___	___	___
Documentation	___	___	___	___	___	___

CREATING EFFECTIVE RESOURCE MATERIALS 7
Materials That Put the Need to Know, Nice to Know, and How to Find At People's Fingertips

All things being equal, people like "stuff." When we walk into a seminar or workshop and we see a lot of neat "stuff," we start the seminar with the feeling that there's going to be something here for us to benefit from. Now, the instructor can quickly demonstrate that that's not true, but the initial impression that we have as participants is that there is something to be gained.

There are at least five benefits of providing resource materials to participants.

1. Enhancing the Educational Offering
Participants can't possibly take complete and accurate notes of everything that happens in the classroom, so handouts can help participants fill in the gaps. The handout can also go beyond the classroom time by providing additional materials that couldn't be covered in the classroom.

2. Enhancing Marketing Opportunities
As trainers, we need to constantly be selling the value of the training that we're delivering. When participants go back to the workplace with well-organized materials that they can show to supervisors and co-workers, those materials are saying, "This seminar is worthwhile."

3. Ensuring Instructor Preparation
When instructors have deadlines for preparing course materials that they'll be using, it helps to ensure preparation. Preparation of handouts and resource materials take time, but it also helps to ensure that the instructor spends time in advance of the class thinking about the content, thinking about the sequence, etc., simply because those affect how the materials are put together.

4. Helping the Instructor Get Through the First Critical Moments of the Class
It is possible to be nervous in starting a new seminar. When resource materials are available, an instructor can take time leading participants

through the materials so that they have an awareness of the overall class and of the materials that are available. This helps the participants get comfortable and also helps the instructor develop some momentum and eliminate any nervousness.

5. Providing a Way of Demonstrating the Instructor's Competency
When the instructor is the one who has prepared the course materials, participants look at those materials, and, without the instructor saying anything verbally, the material shows the participants that the instructor has expertise in this area.

Here's a checklist. Let's take the *Creative Training Techniques Seminar Workbook* as an example of how an effective resource manual could be structured.

Part 1. Table of Contents
On page one, we have a table of contents so that any participant picking up the workbook can say to him or herself, "This is organized." Analytical participants can relax a little bit knowing that there is a structure to the program.

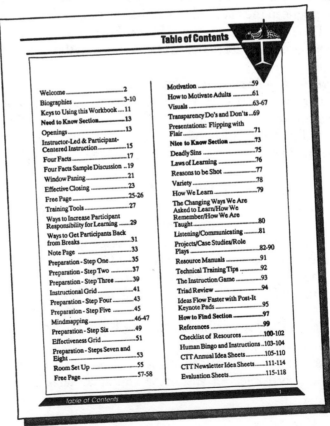

Part 2. Welcome

On page two, we have a welcome letter that helps orient participants to the seminar and gives them an idea of what to expect during the seminar.

Part 3. Credibility

On page three and following, we have biosketches of the trainers. No one is ever as famous or as credible as they'd like to be. Oftentimes in seminars it's not appropriate, because of the size of the group, to provide introductions. For example, you wouldn't have a colleague give an introduction of you to a seminar group that consisted of four people. But a written biosketch can help the participants be aware of what gives this instructor the right to be teaching this seminar. People may not be aware of the years of experience or the specialized training that you may have gone through in order to get ready to do this seminar. A biosketch can help develop your credibility.

Biography

Robert W. Pike, CSP - President

Robert W. Pike, CSP
President

Robert has developed and implemented training program for business, industry, government, and the professions since 1969. Beginning as a representative for Master Education Industries, he received nine promotions in three and one half years, to Senior Vice President. His responsibilities included developing an intensive three week Master Training Academy covering all phases of sales training, management development, communications, motivation/platform skills and business operations. During his five years as Vice President of Personal Dynamics, Inc., that company grew from less than 4,000 enrollments per year to more than 80,000. He pioneered undergraduate and graduate credit on a national basis.

As president of Resources for Organizations, Inc., Creative Training Techniques International, Inc., and The Resources Group, Inc., Bob leads sessions over 150 days per year covering topics of leadership, attitudes, motivation, communication, decision-making, problem-solving, personal and organizational effectiveness, conflict management, team building and managerial productivity. More than 50,000 trainers have attended the Creative Training Techniques® workshop. As a consultant Bob has worked with such organizations as Pfizer, Upjohn, Caesars Boardwalk Regency, Exhibitor Magazine, Hallmark Cards Inc. and IBM. A member of the American Society for Training and Development (ASTD) since 1972, Bob has been active in many capacities including three National Conference Design Committees, Director of Special Interest Groups, and member of the National Board of Directors.

An outstanding speaker, Bob has presented at regional and national ASTD and Training Conferences to crowds ranging from 300-1100 people. Bob was recently granted the professional designation of Certified Speaking Professional (CSP) by the National Speakers Association (NSA). This designation has been earned by only 170 of the more than 3800 members of the NSA.

Since 1980 he has been listed in the Who's Who in the Midwest and in the current edition of Who's Who in Finance and Industry. Over the years Bob has contributed to magazines like Training, The Personnel Administrator and The Self Development Journal. He is editor of the Creative Training Techniques newsletter. He is author of The Creative Training Techniques Handbook, Developing, Marketing and Promoting Successful Seminars and Workshops, and Improving Managerial Productivity.

3

Part 4. Workbook Orientation

Part four is a workbook orientation. In our workbook, we include a page entitled "Keys to Using this Workbook" which lets users know that there are three parts to the workbook. The first section, "Need to Know," is on the white pages and those 72 pages are going to be covered very thoroughly during the seminar. The second section, "Nice to Know," is on the purple pages. They're supplemental, and depending on the needs of the group, some of those pages will be used in the seminar. It's important to note that any partial pages are in the "Need to Know" pages, whereas the "Nice to Know" pages can stand alone. People are not going to be frustrated by finding blanks and wondering what those blanks represent.

The third section, "How to Find," is located in the yellow pages. In other words, these are resources that are going to be useful to them later and are easily accessible.

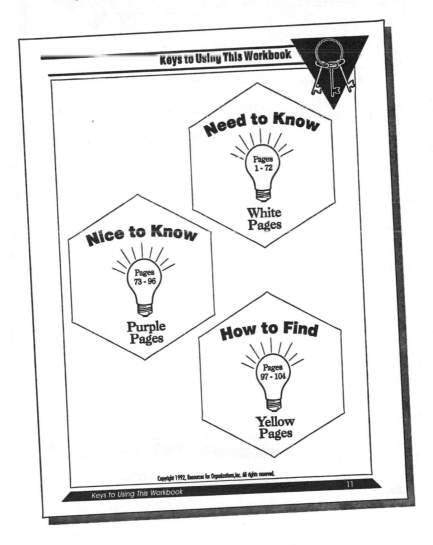

Keys to Using This Workbook

Need to Know
Pages 1 - 72
White Pages

Nice to Know
Pages 73 - 96
Purple Pages

How to Find
Pages 97 - 104
Yellow Pages

11

Keys to Using This Workbook

Part 5. Partial Handouts

Here is the handout we use for openings. It includes key blanks that need to be filled in. The instructor uses computer graphics, flip charts, or transparencies to provide the participants with the key words. This way the participant can focus on what's happening in the class, has a track to run on with the partial hand-out and, if the participant chooses, needs only to write in the key word to have the hand-out be complete, yet frequently will take many more notes.

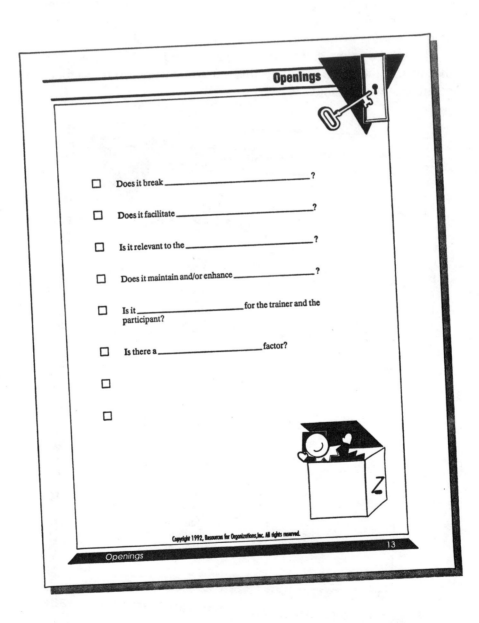

Openings

☐ Does it break _____?

☐ Does it facilitate _____?

☐ Is it relevant to the _____?

☐ Does it maintain and/or enhance _____?

☐ Is it _____ for the trainer and the participant?

☐ Is there a _____ factor?

☐

☐

Openings

13

Part 6. Note Pages

In the front part of the resource material, every left page is a note page so that if participants need more space than the actual hand-out they're writing on, they can take additional notes right next to the hand-out that they're working on. At the bottom of the note page, since the participants receive a copy of *The Creative Training Techniques Handbook*, the pages that relate to the hand-out are highlighted so that if they want to go beyond what's covered in class they know exactly where to find it in *The Creative Training Techniques Handbook*.

Notes

CTT Handbook, pp. 106 - 108

12

Part 7. Activity Guide Sheets

Some people can hear verbal instructions and completely understand what needs to be done. Others find it much more comfortable to hear the instructions, but then have the instructions in front of them.

There is an activity that we do in Creative Training Techniques called Four "Facts." The first part of the activity is completed individually. The instructor reads the instructions out loud and then models the instructions by providing four facts about him or herself. Participants then list their own facts on the page. A group leader is then chosen and leads the group through the activity based on the instructions given. Once again, the instructor has given these instructions verbally, perhaps picked out one group and walked the entire room through how the activity would work with this one group, and then has each of the groups in the seminar do the activity based on the steps that are listed.

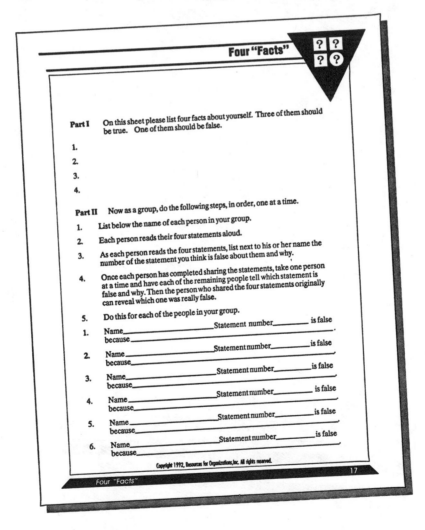

Four "Facts"

Part I On this sheet please list four facts about yourself. Three of them should be true. One of them should be false.

1.

2.

3.

4.

Part II Now as a group, do the following steps, in order, one at a time.

1. List below the name of each person in your group.

2. Each person reads their four statements aloud.

3. As each person reads the four statements, list next to his or her name the number of the statement you think is false about them and why.

4. Once each person has completed sharing the statements, take one person at a time and have each of the remaining people tell which statement is false and why. Then the person who shared the four statements originally can reveal which one was really false.

5. Do this for each of the people in your group.

1. Name_____Statement number_____ is false

because_____.

2. Name_____Statement number_____ is false

because_____.

3. Name_____Statement number_____ is false

because_____.

4. Name_____Statement number_____ is false

because_____.

5. Name_____Statement number_____ is false

because_____.

6. Name_____Statement number_____ is false

because_____.

17

Four "Facts"

Part 8. Follow-Up Discussion Sheets

Almost every activity that is done in a seminar needs to be processed in some way. Sometimes that processing can simply be done verbally through a discussion. At other times, it is more helpful to let smaller groups within the seminar discuss what happened and why, and discussion sheets can really help make that much easier. Once the Four "Facts" activity is over, participants are then given the Four "Facts" discussion sheet which is then used in small groups.

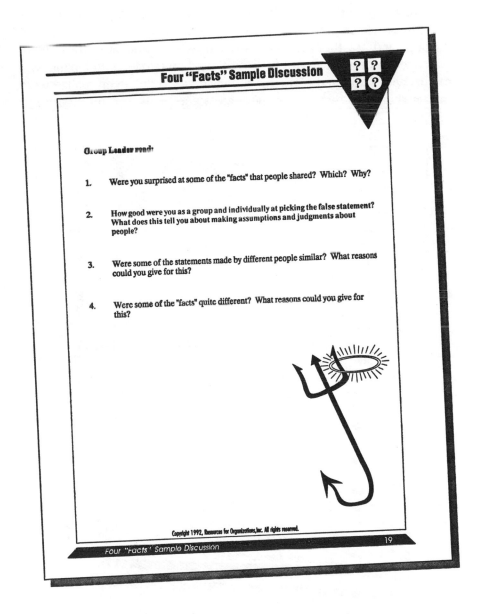

Four "Facts" Sample Discussion

Group Leader read:

1. Were you surprised at some of the "facts" that people shared? Which? Why?

2. How good were you as a group and individually at picking the false statement? What does this tell you about making assumptions and judgments about people?

3. Were some of the statements made by different people similar? What reasons could you give for this?

4. Were some of the "facts" quite different? What reasons could you give for this?

Four "Facts" Sample Discussion   19

Part 9. Reference Lists

Reference lists can be given complete or they can be developed by participants themselves. We give people a training tools sheet so that as they go through the seminar and notice a training tool that they like, they can create their own reference list in the workbook. Examples of tools that might appear on this list are Mr. Sketch™ markers, special water-based markers that don't bleed through on the flip charts, 3M™ tape flags that can be used to create reference points that are easy to get back to in the manual, and perhaps checklists in the seminar.

We have seven different methods that we can use to get participants back from breaks on time, so we give them to participants in the form of a checklist and ask them to discuss when, where, and how these were used to get them back from break on time. Sometimes, participants will come up with additional ways that the instructor didn't even realize were being used and for that reason there are some blanks on the bottom of the page.

Part 10. Graphs

In the seminar we spend time looking at an instructional design grid that was part of an article that several of us contributed to the *1987 University Associates Annual for Developing Human Resources.* The diagram, or grid, can help to convey a lot of information in a very condensed space. When talking about room set-ups, diagrams are much more helpful to give participants than simply giving them a verbal explanation.

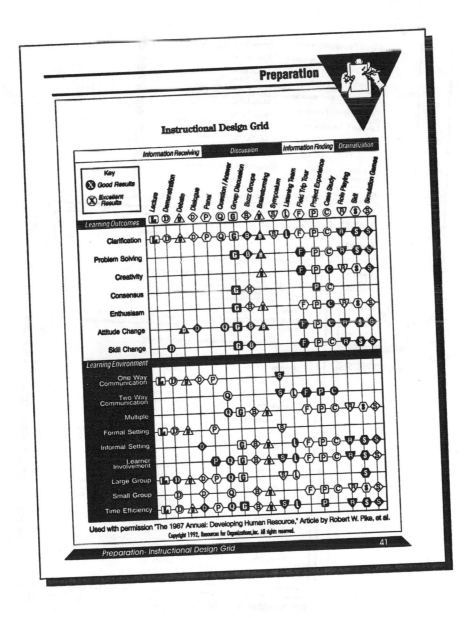

Part 11. Reference Sheets

Once information is covered in the seminar, it may be helpful to provide a summary of the things that have been covered, or a bonus sheet that covers that information, plus additional information such as the list of "Transparency Do's and Don'ts" below that we include in the workbook.

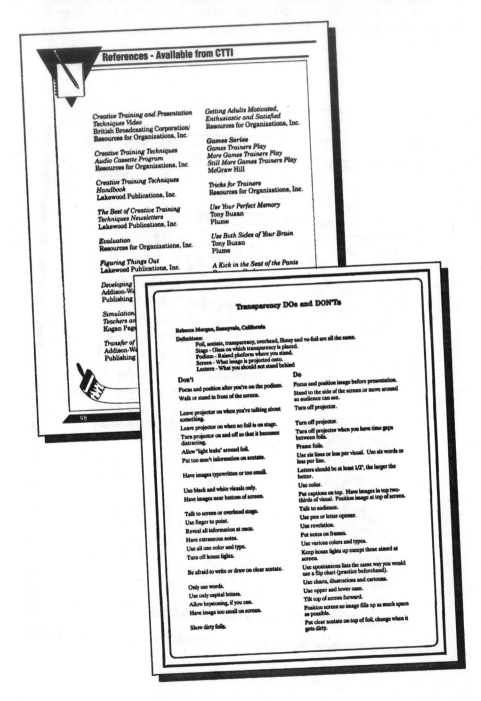

PRESENTATION TECHNIQUES

8

How to Build and Deliver
Powerful Presentations

What makes a powerful presentation? Just what can we do to get people to listen and respond in a positive manner to what we have to say? Each of us has had the experience of being captivated by a presentation, one that would have held our attention indefinitely. We've also probably shared the experience of being "trapped" in a presentation that felt as though it lasted ten times longer than necessary. So how do we design presentations and training programs that fit into the first category and avoid the pitfalls that put us in the second category?

My operational definition of a presentation is: the systematic discussion, explanation, or demonstration of skills, knowledge, or attitudes. A presentation is not necessarily a lecture, though lecture may be part of it. A powerful presentation enables participants to expand skills, reinforce or change attitudes, and gain new knowledge. For the trainer, presentations are not limited to training programs. There are executive briefings and overviews, problem-solving meetings, budget meetings, meetings to consider proposals for new programs, reports, etc. Presentation is a part of all of these. Some presentations are delivered on short notice, but a knowledge of presentation formats can help the presenter use even a short amount of preparation time effectively. Now, what are the keys to building powerful presentations?

First, let's remember that every person in our program is going to be tuned to two radio stations— *WII-FM: What's In It For Me?* and *MMFI-AM: Make Me Feel Important About Myself.* Whatever we design and deliver must be based on those two points. Since all the participants will be asking, "What's in it for me?," we must, in preparing our presentation, continually reinforce the payoff for those participants if we're going to achieve the impact we want. Furthermore, we want to build the confidence of our participants so we can ensure the transfer, back on the job, of the skills they've learned and the knowledge they've developed. That means keeping the focus and spotlight on the participants as much as possible. The greater their sense of accomplishment in the class, the greater the transfer back on the job.

Where, we must ask ourselves, do we want to be at the end of the presentation? Too many presentations just sort of dribble off inconclusively; in others, the instructor races through the latter part of the content because time is running out. A strong conclusion is a must for any training program and, as a matter of fact, for every segment of a training program. It is not enough to capture the attention of participants at the beginning and/or to deliver strong content in the middle; it is also imperative to have a strong wrap-up that drives home the point(s) you've made.

Training programs can last for days, weeks, or even months, but the length of each presentation must be in tune with the attention span of the participants. If the focus of our training is results, as it should be, then we must work within limits appropriate to what participants can absorb.

Try this little test on yourself, carefully following the instructions in order to derive maximum benefit from this illustration. Clearly read aloud the following series of numbers:

$$6, 9, 12, 4, 14, 7, 5, 8, 11$$

Now jot down your answers to these three questions without looking back at the series of numbers.

1. What was the first number in the sequence?
2. What was the last number in the sequence?
3. What was the middle number in the sequence?

In my seminars, 95 percent of the participants usually recall the first number correctly, 65 to 90 percent correctly recall the last number, but 20 percent or less correctly recall the middle number. This would indicate that people remember beginnings and endings rather than what comes in the middle. One conclusion for presenters is to design programs that have more compelling beginnings and endings—and to find ways to reinforce the middle.

People have limited short-term memories. Have you ever looked up a seven-digit phone number, dialed, heard a busy signal, hung up, and tried to redial—only to realize you'd already forgotten the number you had just looked up and dialed? For most of us, it's a common experience; once we get beyond seven "bits" of information, we start to lose that information. Perhaps that's why there's so much emphasis on the "30-second sound bite" in political advertising. And why most commercials last 30 seconds or less.

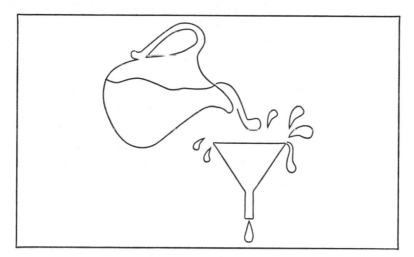

To accommodate participants' limited short-term memories, we should present a limited amount of new information that can be absorbed before adding more information. Imagine pouring liquid through a funnel. If we pour too fast, the liquid spills over and is lost. But if we pour either at a rate less than or equal to the maximum, we'll prevent spillage. Or we can stop periodically to allow the liquid to drain before we continue. Here— and in the presentations—the delivery rate and the amount delivered are key.

As mentioned earlier, in his book *Use Both Sides of Your Brain,* Tony Buzan estimates that the average adult can listen with *understanding* for 90 minutes but with *retention* for only 20 minutes. To me, that means that I need a distinct change-up, or change of pace, at least every 20 minutes in order to create a new learning cycle. Another illustration: Imagine pouring liquid from a container holding nine quarts into one that holds two quarts. After you pour out two quarts, you must empty your smaller container and begin the process again. As trainers, we often reach the "two-quart" limit with our participants but keep on "pouring" because there's so much to cover. Just because they're listening, nodding, and smiling doesn't mean we've achieved our goals of retention and application.

Earlier, I mentioned Albert Mehrabian's research on retention: When people are exposed to an idea one time, they retain 10 percent or less of it after 30 days. Yet when they are exposed to the same idea six times, with interval reinforcement, their retention is 90 percent at the end of 30 days. The implication for trainers is that we need to build opportunities for review and reinforcement into our presentations.

PRESENTATION DESIGN METHODS

Several models can be used for designing presentations. Which method you choose will depend on the type of information you cover, the amount of time you have, the experience level of your participants, and whether you want your participants to attain familiarity, mastery, or something in between.

Since 1969, I've used all of the following outlines to build and deliver powerful presentations.

Problem-Solving Approach

A. History of the problem—Why is there a problem? Where did it come from? What makes it a problem? Whom does it affect?

B. Current condition of the problem—What's the status of the problem now? How widespread is it? How likely is it to continue? What are the consequences if we don't act?

C. Possible solutions—What are the alternatives? What are the advantages and disadvantages of each? How quickly can each be implemented? What is the likelihood of success?

D. Possible solutions—What do these solutions mean to your listeners? How does each affect them? (Remember, they're tuned to *WII-FM!*) How does it affect others, especially others important to them?

E. The best solution and why—Given all the available information, what's the best course of action to take?

F. Call to action

If your time is short, present most of the information in the preceding approach in hand-out form and follow this abbreviated outline.

A. Problem

B. Solution

C. Call to action

Here's an example of how I used the shortened form of the problem-solving approach myself.

A. Problem

I found myself stuck on the same opening for every training program I delivered. It seemed to be worn-out—both for me and my participants.

B. Solution

Then I asked myself, "What makes an opening effective?," and I came up with three things.

• It breaks preoccupation.

• It facilitates networking—and generally anything involving a small-group approach does that.

• It makes a point about the training. If the opening I use helps people discover a deficiency of knowledge or execution, helps them recognize the existence of a problem, or helps them open their minds and be less judgmental and/or hasty, then I've succeeded.

C. Call to Action

By asking—and answering—that question about openings, I could begin to deliver more powerful, meaningful openings to my training programs and presentations.

Past, Present, Future Approach

This approach is especially appropriate for extemporaneous presentations, especially those that chronicle personal experience or knowledge.

- *Past*—What was it, or what were you, like in the past in terms of the topic at hand? For example: In the past, I had difficulty knowing where to start when developing a presentation. My brain seemed to freeze, and I couldn't get my pencil to move. Everything was bottled up inside, out of reach.

- *Present*—What is it, or what are you, like now? For example: Now things flow more smoothly when I develop a presentation. By applying brainstorming techniques and reviewing different outline formats, ideas start to come, and I can begin to fill in the blanks.

- *Future*—What will happen in the future? For example: In the future, I plan to add new outlines to increase my options. I also plan to look for stories, illustrations, and poems that can spice up my presentations so I can continue to increase my effectiveness.

New-Twist Approach

    A An old idea
    B. A new twist on an old idea
    C. How you found it
    D. How it worked for you
    E. How your listeners can use it
    F. Call to action

Here's an example of how I used the new-twist approach myself.

A. An old idea—For as long as I can remember, I've used flip charts, especially in brainstorming sessions I facilitated. But the sessions seemed to bog down when the ideas started to come fast and furiously.

B. A new twist on an old idea—Then I started asking two or more participants to volunteer as recorders. They would do the writing, leaving me free to facilitate the discussion.

C. How I found the idea—When I was a participant myself in a brainstorming session, I observed a facilitator who used a volunteer to record ideas. The technique kept things moving fairly briskly, but, I thought, "If one works reasonably well, why not use two volunteers to really speed things along?"

D. How it worked for you—My brainstorming sessions haven't been the same since. They move as quickly as the ideas surface.

E. How your listeners can use the idea—When asking for volunteers, clarify what you're asking them to do. I try to make it less intimidating to volunteer by joking, "If you can't spell a word at least two ways, you're not being creative." Also, give each volunteer recorder two markers of different colors; printing alternating ideas in different colors helps people see each one separately.

F. Call to action—Just stock up on markers, and the next time you're tempted to pick them up, ask for not one volunteer but two!

THEORY AND SKILL SESSIONS

In the mid-1980s, I worked with Mike Berger, who was then director of the Corporate Learning Institute at Vanderbilt University, in developing a Technical Education Forum for IBM. Mike said that every theory or skill session should MOVE participants in the opening and RECAP for participants at the close. I think it's sage advice.

Motivate	**R**eview
Orient and preview	**E**licit
in**V**estigate	**C**onnect
Explain objectives	**A**nswer
	Punctuate

Eight Dynamite Motivators

1. DESCRIBE AN INCIDENT

I want you to imagine it's a warm August evening, the night of your organization's annual awards banquet. For four years, you've worked hard, been loyal to your company, and, over time, made an increasingly greater contribution at work. You're excited because you're certain (or almost certain) that tonight your efforts will be recognized.

You've flown to Denver, picked up a luxury rental car, and enjoyed a leisurely drive to Colorado Springs, 90 miles to the south. The majestic scenery of the Colorado Rockies unfolds on your right as you drive. At the off-ramp into Colorado Springs, you exit and proceed up a wide, tree-lined boulevard. Ahead of you looms the fabulous Broadmoor, one of America's few five-star, five-diamond, five-everything hotels.

Your car door is opened promptly by the doorman, and you're ushered up the marble steps. At the top, you begin a long walk down the marble-floored, wood-paneled corridor leading to the ballroom. Fifteen-foot-high mirrors reflect your progress. Gold and crystal chandeliers light the way.

You enter the ballroom and join 400 of your coworkers. Every moment of the evening is fantastic. The dinner is superb, the service exquisite. You almost want to pinch yourself. It's too good to be true.

Finally, the awards begin. As the presentations continue, you realize that either you are going to be recognized as your company's outstanding contributor—or you're going home empty handed.

The company president steps to the podium to present the final award. When he glances your way, you realize instantly that tonight's your night. The award is yours.

The president begins. "Our recipient doesn't know this, but four years ago, every manager he'd had had recommended his termination. The feeling was, this person could never live up to the high standards we set in our organization. Only I was able to see his potential. So I began to act as a sort of mentor to him, carefully laying out a step-by-step development plan. I spent hours of one-on-one time, sharing my wisdom and insights and explaining to him the ideas, concepts, and techniques that have made me a leader in our industry. As our recipient began to implement my development plan—never wavering, never deviating, never questioning the course I'd set—the results became obvious. This past year especially, my plan has paid dividends as this person outperformed all others in our organization. It's my privilege to recognize our company's outstanding contributor..."

As you hear your name called, how do you feel?

When I've described this scenario and asked this question, I've heard such answers as: "Cheated," "Angry," "I'd feel like crawling under a rock," and "I'd feel like giving the award back to the president; he obviously thinks it's his." Almost everyone who is asked to comment on this incident feels motivated to offer his or her reaction. And that's the whole point; you want to motivate participants to become involved in your presentation.

2. ASK FOR A SHOW OF HANDS

But the show of hands must be meaningful. If people want to look around to see who else has a hand up, then you've probably asked a good question. Here are two I've used.

1. How many of you have ever observed a "dynamic duo" in your class? You know, two people who walk in together, sit down together, fold their arms together, and both give you body language that says, "I don't want to be here, so this better be good." Can I see a show of hands? (Wait for a response.) Good, that means you've been in training longer than a week. (This usually gets a laugh.)

2. In one opening activity, I ask participants to interview other participants in a scavenger-hunt type of activity. The objective is to find people for whom various statements are true. For example, find someone in this room who:

- Was an only child
- Is a downhill skier
- Reads *Popular Mechanics*
- Drives a pick-up
- Has been a trainer for five or more years
- Has worked for three or more companies in his or her career

I ask participants to check the two or three items they think will be hardest to find among the group. When the activity is over, I ask people to volunteer which items they checked, and then I ask people to raise their hands if the item was true for them. For example: "How many of you are downhill skiers? Let's have a show of hands." People are often quite surprised by the number of hands that go up in response.

3. ASK A QUESTION
We're so conditioned to answer questions that we often answer even those we may not want to answer. The only thing we're more conditioned to answer than a question is the telephone. (Try not answering yours the next time it rings!) You can direct the question to an individual, leave it to an individual to volunteer, or elicit a group response by a show of hands.

4. MAKE A PROMISE
One that I make in the Creative Training Techniques seminar is: "By the end of these two days, you'll have at least five ways you can improve your next training program without redesigning one handout or creating one new visual." That promise always gets the participants' attention. I check back with them from time to time to see if they think that I'm fulfilling my promise and to elicit specific techniques that they're going to use. This serves both to demonstrate my intentions and to encourage periodic review.

5. GET THEM LAUGHING
Notice I didn't say, "Tell a joke." Humor in this context should always make a point. I believe that natural, timely humor is the most effective. When I ask the question about the "dynamic duo" and then say, after the participants respond with a show of hands, "That means you've been in training longer than a week!," they almost always laugh because the humor has a real-life basis.

Effective, natural humor that comes from our own life experience does three things.

1. It makes a point.

2. It shares a story or illustration participants have never heard before because it comes from our personal experience.

3. It draws our audience closer to us because we all can identify with the foibles and triumphs of others.

Humor should fit naturally and logically into a presentation. Don't use an illustration just because it's funny; it must be relevant as well.

You don't *have* to be funny. People aren't expecting Bob Hope, Bill Cosby, or Joan Rivers. They expect you and what you have to share on the topic at hand. If you do decide to use stories or jokes outside your experience, make sure they're appropriate for the group. Stories that someone in business would find amusing may not draw a chuckle from a construction worker, and vice versa. If you select humor that's not funny, you may find yourself trying to make it funny with accents and theatrics. Don't. Both you and your audience will regret it.

Every occupation is filled with its own kind of humor. And those who share that occupation can identify with it. Your stories don't have to be embellished, embroidered, or delivered with an accent. By simply sharing an amusing story, you'll have the audience laughing with you—and getting the point.

Over time, you may have repeat participants from previous programs who may not find your stories funny the second time around. So keep looking for fresh stories and experiences to share, and avoid those that have become time-worn. People who hear you repeat an illustration they've already heard umpteen times may decide that you're lazy and don't care.

Finally, consider these rules of thumb about humor.

- It's wonderful when you know how and when to use it, disastrous when you don't.
- It's a tool to drive home ideas, not a substitute for them.
- Use humor based on caring, never on contempt.
- If the story is going to be "on" someone, it should be "on" you.
- Forget off-color humor or humor that uses offensive language.
- Be careful about any story involving race, religion, sex, and politics. When in doubt, don't use it.

6. MAKE A PROVOCATIVE STATEMENT

I've said things like: "There are four reasons a trainer ought to be shot on the spot!" That usually gets people's attention. They didn't think there was one reason for shooting a trainer. (And there probably isn't, but the statement sure commands attention!)

7. CITE AN UNUSUAL STATISTIC

I recently used some facts that I'd come across in a study. They showed that a person starting work at age 25 and working full-time until 65 spends an average of 16.8 percent of his or her time on the job. I wanted to show the advantage to an organization of helping employees develop skills that can be used both on and off the job. If people spend 82.8 percent of their time off the job and if they have problems, it certainly affects performance —negatively. And if things are going smoothly, it also affects performance —positively. But when I used the statistics, they were challenged. What were the demographics? What companies? Where? How was the sampling done?

So now I use another approach when citing those unusual statistics. I involve the participants by saying, "An average person starts work full-time at 25 and works full-time through age 65. Write down what percent of that person's time you guess is spent on the job. We're not talking about how productive the person is, just whether or not he or she is physically present."

After a moment, I ask for a show of hands. "How many of you think a person spends 90 percent-plus of his or her time on the job?" I work down to 10 percent by 10 percent increments. The average of this tally usually is roughly 40+ percent. I draw a circle on the board and split it into a 60 percent piece and a 40 percent piece.

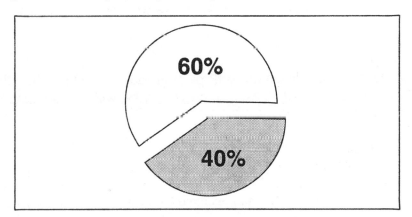

I then ask, "If a person has problems in 60 percent of his or her life, how likely is that to affect the other 40 percent?" The answer usually is "a lot." Then I write 365 (the number of days in a year) on the board. But the average person doesn't work weekends, so we subtract 102 days. Then we subtract the average number of paid holidays—10. Next, the number of vacation days in an average year—about 15. The number of sick or personal-leave days? Generally 6. Subtracting all these from 365 gives us 232 days. The average person works 8 hours a day, so we divide by 3 to get 77, which is approximately 21 percent of 365.

Remember, the perception was 40 percent, but the statistic is 16.8 percent. Using their own data, the participants got close to the provocative statistic. Now, the final question: "If the average person spends 80 percent of his or her time off the job and if he or she has a problem, how likely is that to affect performance on the job?" If the answer is "a lot" at 60 percent (and it always seems to be), how much greater the impact when their data show 80 percent!

8. USE A VISUAL AID OR PROP
I've used all kinds of them—cookies, potatoes, pointers for overhead transparencies that looked like small human hands. All of these grab attention and gain interest.

And they motivate, too. Because they create curiosity, and because people want one—of whatever it is. They may not know what the objects are, but they'll start thinking of ways to contribute to get one.

Orient and Preview

Having participants answer and discuss the following questions will help reinforce the importance of what you're about to cover. Why is this material important? Why have you been chosen to be here? Why was this material chosen? How will you be able to use this material? What's the road map for the time we're together? Where are we going to start? Where will we end?

Investigate

What level of knowledge do participants already have about the subject? What is the extent of their experience? How soon will they be using what they're about to learn?

Explain the Objectives

It's important that participants enter a theory or a skill session knowing what's expected of them. What will they know when the session is over? How will their feelings or attitudes have changed? What will they be able to do?

Review

We want to review without necessarily calling it review. I've used a variety of techniques to do this. Sometimes I have participants keep track of "action ideas" for use back on the job. They start by sharing them in small groups, which then feed back to the entire group. This process covers most of the content. I then hit any additional points I want to reinforce.

I've also had participants make up test questions they think people ought to be able to answer after the presentation. I split the group into at least three subgroups, each of which develops a test. The tests are then rotated to a second group, which reviews the test for completeness, clarity, and fairness, and then to a third group, which takes the test.

Elicit New Ideas

What new applications do people see for the content? What problems does it solve? Perhaps someone will offer a better way of doing what's been done or, at least, a creative alternative.

Connect to the Future

What's the on-the-job application? What are the possible barriers to application? What strategies can be used to overcome the barriers? How could the participants support one another in the application of the new skills and knowledge?

Answer Questions

But I never ask, "Are there any questions?" I usually break the group into subgroups and give them two to three minutes to go over the content and develop two or three questions they'd like to ask. This allows for another review. Many of the questions will be answered within the group itself. The questions that eventually are asked are of general interest to the entire group.

Punctuate Finish

We don't want the conclusion just to trail off. Nor do we want it rushed— by throwing out lots of content in the closing minutes just so we can say it was covered. We want to end with punch, with impact. Here are seven ways to do just that.

1. Summarize the total program in a few well-chosen words.
2. Restate the main points.
3. Present a call to action.

For example, you might say, "Involvement is important to building retention and ensuring on-the-job application. You've experienced it here. You've actively participated in discovering ways to involve your own participants. You can generate the same energy in your own classes if you'll keep applying the techniques you've been using."

4. Use humor.

David Peoples, one of IBM's three consulting instructors, frequently closes his presentations in this good-humor note:

> *I fully realize that I have not succeeded in answering all your questions. Indeed, I feel I have not answered any of them completely. The answers I have found only serve to raise a whole new set of questions, which only lead to more problems, some of which we weren't even aware were problems. To sum it all up, I feel we are just as confused as ever in some ways, but I believe we are confused at a higher level and about more important things.*

If the presentation has been heavy with content, this serves to lighten the mood. Wrap things up on a high note.

5. Close with a quote.

For example: "Remember that Confucius said, in 451 B.C., 'What I hear, I forget; what I see, I may remember; but what I do, I understand.' It applies today. Involvement is the key to realizing results."

Another example. "Remember what you've experienced in this time we've had together. As C.S. Lewis, the English philosopher, said, 'A man with an experience is never at the mercy of a man with an argument.' You know that the techniques you've been using do work. We haven't just talked about things; we've done them. Keep on broadening your experience."

6. Recite a poem.

An example. "We've been talking about giving recognition, encouragement, and approval, about letting people know they count. With that in mind, I'd like to close with a poem by Charles Jarvis.

Life's a bother, life's a hurry,
Life's a busy crowded way,
Good intentions go astray.
I had a friend the other day.
I haven't any more. He passed away.
I meant to write, to phone, to call.
I didn't do any of those at all.
I only hope that he can now see
How much his friendship meant to me.
Life's a busy crowded way,
Good intentions go astray.

Let's not let our good intentions go astray. Let's show appreciation now to the people who count—on the job, at home, in the community."

7. Offer an anecdote.

For example, "We've been talking about managing and coaching people. I believe that it's important to support people, but we can't do their jobs for them. If you and I will support our people by using the skills we've been developing here, then we'll have fulfilled our responsibilities.

"I'll never forget my first management position. I had responsibility for a field sales force, and I was determined that none of my people would fail. After all, I had personally experienced every failure behavior, so I could help them avoid all the traps I had fallen into.

"One day, one of the first people I had recruited called me and said, 'I quit. I can't do this.' I was in shock for two days. Where had I gone wrong? What didn't I do? After a lot of soul searching, I realized I had done everything I could. This fellow had received three weeks of intensive training at the beginning. He had come into the home office for an additional two days of training after 60 days in the field and after 120 days in the field. We had done field selling together. We had received bi-weekly mailings of additional support material. He had audiotapes to reinforce all the training he had received. He had audiovisual aids to help him make his presentations. I had, to the best of my ability, done everything I could but do his job for him.

"If we'll take that approach in coaching, guiding, and counseling our people, we'll be effective managers. But we have to balance our responsibility with the fact that the people we manage must respond to their own opportunities as well. We'll never be able to do *that* for them."

THE BODY OF THEORY AND SKILL SESSIONS

While the openings and closings of theory and skill sessions can follow the same pattern, there are differences in the body of the session.

For a theory session, we want to:
- Explain the theory;
- Activate the participants, or involve them in an activity so they can experience the theory in practice;
- Summarize the theory; and
- Conclude the session.

For a skill session, we want to:
- Show the skill—performing it in its entirety without commentary;
- Show and tell—performing the skill with a running commentary about each step;
- Practice (participants practice the skill on their own); and
- Provide feedback so participants can learn how they've performed the skill.

Effective Openings

An effective opening announces four things to your participants.

1. Your time will be used well here.
2. I understand who you are, including your background and the expertise and experience you bring.
3. Because I respect you, I'm prepared.
4. I know my content by both training and experience.

Ten Tips on Effective Openings

1. Open with energy, enthusiasm, and animation.

No one is interested in listening to another dull, dry, listless presentation. Project your interest and enthusiasm. Bring vitality and intensity to the presentation. Challenge your participants.

2. Don't apologize.

Prepare so thoroughly that you don't need to. Remember, if you feel you must apologize, probably 85 percent of your audience won't know what you're apologizing for, unless you point it out, and the other 15 percent won't be affected by it.

3. Make eye contact.

There is power in eye contact. To build that power, focus on the eyes of one individual. Look at that person eyeball-to-eyeball, and move about the room establishing the same intense eye contact. Don't stare at the floor, the ceiling, the walls, or the back of the room.

4. Be "others-oriented."

Instead of being self-conscious, be "others-conscious." If you focus on putting your message across, delivering your content, persuading and influencing your listeners, you won't have to worry about whether or not you're putting on a "good performance." People will appreciate and respect you if you make a sincere, honest effort to benefit them. Thomas Carlyle said over 100 years ago, "Care not for the reward of your speaking, but simply, and with undivided mind, for the truth of your speaking."

5. Give the audience an overview.

Remember to "tell them what you're going to tell them, and then tell them what you told them." Early on, lay the foundation for the material that you'll cover. Define key terms. Establish a common ground with your audience.

6. Focus attention.

Ask participants, "What are the key questions that need to be answered? What makes them urgent? What's the first question?"

7. Be open.

For the most part, the audience should know exactly who you are, what your attitudes are about the subject, and why you feel confident to handle it. They should be able to sense your sincere interest in communicating and sharing your ideas with them.

8. Be aware of your appearance.

How you look can either encourage people to be receptive to your message or discourage them from heeding it. Appearances *do* count and so do first impressions.

- *Clothing*—Are you dressed professionally? Are you properly groomed? I believe that how we dress shows our respect for the participants. Dress a little more formally than you think you need to. It's a lot easier to dress down if you're slightly overdressed, by removing a jacket, rolling up sleeves, etc., then it is to try to dress up a too-casual outfit.

- *Gestures*—Do you use your hands and your head comfortably? Are your gestures compatible with what you are saying?

- *Facial Expressions*—Is your face animated? Does it communicate an interest in your audience and your subject?
- *Posture*—Do you stand alert and erect, without being stiff?
- *Body Movement*—Do your movements and changes in body positions serve a communication purpose? Do they focus attention on the subject at hand?

9. Be aware of your voice.

Kathleen Hessert, president of Communication Concepts in Charlotte, North Carolina, is a specialist in executive communications. After years as a journalist, newscaster, and anchorperson, she has developed a presentation titled "How You Sound Is So Awful I Can't Hear What You Say." Her point is that a presenter's voice can significantly affect an audience's receptivity.

- *Tone*—Do you communicate enthusiasm, seriousness, interest, excitement in your tone of voice?
- *Enunciation*—Do you clearly pronounce, or enunciate, each word, or do you slur or skip certain sounds?
- *Pace, Speed*—Do you time pauses? Do you fill those vocal pauses with um's and ah's? Do you speak fluently or haltingly? Are you too fast or too slow?
- *Word Choice*—Do you use the appropriate words to convey your thoughts? Will your audience be lost because you use words with which they're unfamiliar? Will they be insulted because you define words they already know? Remember "Goldilocks and the Three Bears": Not too hot, not too cold, just right. Your word choice should be the same—not too difficult, not too easy, but just right.

10. Establish and maintain audience contact.

Do you reach out and figuratively touch the audience? Do you establish rapport that will help them identify with your thoughts and ideas?

Building the Middle of a Presentation

SUPPORT

Build support for points that the audience may not fully understand or fully agree with. It's important to support your ideas, first, when the audience is skeptical of the truth or value of an idea and, second, when you're presenting a concept that is difficult to understand.

You might consider using some of the following means of support.

1. *Figures*—Numerical representations of facts
2. *Statistics*—Express factual relationships based on numbers
3. *Facts*—Statements about present or past realities that are verifiable, either by third-party support or by direct observation

4. *Definitions*—Inquiries into understanding the nature of something, usually by going from general to specific—e.g., "A ranch-style house [term] is a type of building [general class] that consists of only one level [particular qualities]."

5. *Anecdotes*—Stories or experiences that are used to illustrate a point but not necessarily prove it

6. *Examples*—Representative instances that prove or clarify a general statement

7. *Illustrations*—More detailed examples that generally offer more specific clarification, point by point

8. *Authorities*—Reliable, recognized sources other than yourself who support your point

9. *Analogies*—Descriptions of a set of similar conditions that shed additional light on the subject being discussed

People often remember vivid illustrations, examples, anecdotes, etc., longer than even the key points they are intended to illustrate. If you speak only in broad, general terms, you may be indicating to your audience that you're not sure of your facts, that your research was superficial, and that you really didn't prepare your presentation thoroughly. If we don't support what we say with evidence, we may fail to persuade or influence the audience completely.

Unfortunately, it's easy to use slipshod support, to say "Research shows..." or "They say..." or "Everyone knows..." But what "research" and who are "they" and "everyone"? Invariably, at least one or more listeners will ask those questions and reduce the credibility of your presentation. Be accurate; avoid vague generalities. Train yourself to speak and think clearly. When citing examples, use specific names of people, places, and things, when possible and permissible.

Support is effective only when it is relevant, clear, accurate, strong enough to withstand counterarguments, and easy to explain.

TRANSITIONS

There are at least seven transitions we can use to connect the various parts of our presentations.

1. *Questions and Answers*—Allowing participants a minute or two to collect their thoughts and generate questions, whether alone, in pairs, or in small groups, can serve as an effective review, as well as a transition. Place a time limit on this type of Q & A, however. And make the time limit known before the Q & A period begins.

2. *Physical movement*—Moving from one side of the room to another can indicate a transition. And the physical movement of participants themselves can be used as a transition. For example, I often ask participants to stand up after they have jotted down their responses to a question. When

everyone is standing, I ask for several to volunteer their responses. Then everyone is seated. This process not only uses physical movement as a transition, but it gives participants a controlled stretch break.

3. *Use of media*—For example, you haven't used any media, but now you turn to the flip chart. By introducing a new "tool," you signal a transition.

4. *Change of media*—You move from the flip chart, for example, to the overhead projector to indicate a transition.

5. *Mini-summary*—From time to time, I may stop and ask participants to share, either by volunteering individually or in small-group discussions, the action ideas they've picked up so far. If I use small groups, I then ask a leader from each to share one or two of the ideas generated. This mini-summary serves as review, gives me feedback about whether I've driven my key points home, and acts as a transition to the next segment of the program.

6. *Refocus*—At times a participant may sidetrack discussion. I then make a comment such as, "Just before Frank made that comment, what were we talking about?" Someone will name our previous topic. That puts us right back on track without wasting any more time—and without embarrassing the participant.

7. *Pause*—Silence can indicate that we've completed one part of our presentation and are about to move on to another.

QUESTIONS

The first transition technique is Questions and Answers. Let's consider that in a bit more detail.

Asking Them

Questions are great tools for stimulating conversation and guiding communication. Here are some key points to remember in using them in your presentations.

1. Plan your questions. Know, in a general way, what you are going to ask and where in your presentation.

2. Know the purpose of each question. In general, questions either elicit information—e.g., "Where do you live?" or "How many employees are there?"—or opinions—e.g., "How do you like this idea?" or "Do you think this plan will work?"

3. When you ask a question, relate it to your audience's or the individual listener's point of reference and background.

4. Go from general questions to more specific ones.

5. Confine your questions to one topic area at a time.

6. Ask questions that are short, clear, and easy to understand. Don't,

for example, ask a question like this: "Which of the five steps in the selling cycle—prospecting, appointments, presentations, enrollments, and referrals—do you feel is most important?" On paper, this may seem like a simple question, but, asked orally of an individual or an audience, it becomes confusing. If you are going to ask a lengthier question, then illustrate, by use of an overhead or flip chart, the key points. For example, you might use an overhead transparency that would show the key parts of the selling cycle and then ask which is the most important. That way, your audience isn't trying so hard to remember the parts of the cycle that they don't even hear your question.

7. Make logical transitions between your questions.

8. When you're leading a discussion, ask questions of the group first and follow with questions to individuals.

9. Avoid questions that can be answered by a yes or no and questions where the answer is implied. Avoid answering questions before your audience has a chance to. Avoid cross-examining.

10. Once you've asked a question, don't interrupt the person who's responding.

Answering Them

Be sure to listen for both intent (what's meant) as well as content (what's being asked). In other words, listen for the feelings, the emotions behind the question.

Acknowledge each question, and show that you understand by paraphrasing it. If necessary, get clarification. "If I understand what you're asking, it's this:..."

Try to answer the question completely and accurately. Verify the questioner's satisfaction. "Did I say enough about that?" "Did I really tell you everything you wanted me to?" Be ready to give additional proof, support, or clarification of your response.

Avoid these five behaviors when answering questions.

1. Being unresponsive—Even if someone is asking too many questions, don't ignore him or her.

2. Showing that you feel the question is inappropriate, stupid, or ill-timed

3. Diverting the question—If at all possible, answer questions as they come up.

4. Going off on a tangent—When somebody asks a question, don't say, "This reminds me of a time when..." and tell a 10-minute war story. By the time you finish, nobody will remember what the question was.

5. Treating two questions as one—Even if two people ask very similar questions, answer them separately.

TIPS FOR COMMUNICATING IDEAS EFFECTIVELY

1. Present single ideas.

Don't throw too many ideas at your audience at one time. If you do, most of them will get lost. Encourage participants to react to an idea once you've presented it. You might say, for example, "Can you think of a use for this idea?"

2. Get people to "buy off" on one idea before presenting another.

Ask them to respond or react to your ideas so you're sure they understand and accept the material before you go on to another point.

3. Be specific.

Communicate as accurately as possible. Use examples, analogies, illustrations. Avoid generalizations.

4. Respond to emotions.

Encourage people to share not only their thoughts but also their feelings. When a person expresses emotion, try to draw that feeling out by providing praise and empathy. Accept the negative emotions people may have. Look for signs of irritation, confusion, or frustration that may indicate that your participants are not listening, understanding, or accepting the content the way they could be.

5. Share yourself.

Be open to giving all you have and all you know. When you are open to your attendees, they will be open to you. You'll have better, deeper, richer communication from other people when you open yourself to them.

6. Know what you want to say.

Make sure your thoughts and ideas, the points you want to cover, are clear in your mind and that you have a total grasp of the content you want to communicate. If something isn't clear to you, it almost certainly won't be clear to somebody else.

7. Use a logical sequence.

Organize your thoughts and ideas in a sequence—chronological, topical, or from more important to less important—that makes sense to your listeners and enables them to apply what you have to offer.

8. Communicate when people are in the mood to listen.

If people are worried, frustrated, angry, upset, or irritated, don't even try to communicate with them. First, deal with those feelings in an effort to eliminate them.

9. Use a language common to your listeners.

Avoid jargon, unfamiliar terms, difficult words. These may prove to your audience that you're "with it" and/or smart, but they often hinder effective communication and application.

10. Involve your audience.

Draw your audience out by asking for their reactions. Listen attentively when they speak.

11. Give feedback.

When someone says something that can be interpreted several ways, give your interpretation to make sure it matches the speaker's. Don't merely parrot back the remark; paraphrase it, and see if the speaker agrees.

12. Create interest.

Demonstrate the importance of the topic to the attendees. Answer their question "What's in it for me?" Be brief, be specific, and make sure you find common ground by considering the feelings, opinions, and attitudes of your attendees regarding the subject under discussion.

13. Think first, talk second.

A car won't run if there's no gas in the tank, and a speaker can't communicate effectively if there aren't clear thoughts in the brain.

14. Know your aim.

Ask yourself, "What is my purpose in communicating this information?" Be specific. Determine exactly what you want attendees to know or feel or do when you finish.

15. Take into account the total environment whenever you communicate.

Be aware of lighting, the room arrangement, the time of day, and the circumstances under which people are coming to the presentation. That is, are they here voluntarily, or were they ordered to participate?

16. Get the opinions of others.

Ask other people for their feedback and their interpretation of your ideas. Get a clear perspective of how other people actually see the ideas you're trying to communicate. Don't assume you're being clear; get feedback that tells you you're clear.

17. Be aware of intent as well as content.

Your tone of voice, posture, facial expressions, dress, receptivity to the input of others—these all communicate your attitude toward your content and your audience.

18. Follow up.

Feedback tells you that your message has been received. Check to make sure you're actually conveying your content. Encourage feedback and input during the presentation, and then follow up afterwards to make sure you did a satisfactory job.

19. Communicate for long-term, as well as short-term, change.

People often resist change. To ensure that they see not only short-term effects but also long-range benefits of new ideas, actions, and directions, provide information in a way that instills confidence, not fear.

20. Make sure actions and attitudes support your presentation.

Heed these words: "What you are speaks so loudly I can't hear what you say." Be sure that your actions and attitudes support your words.

21. Be a good listener.

Very few people are looking for a good talker, but they are looking for someone who will listen. And they will give a lot of power to that rare individual.

Group presentations give you a tremendous opportunity for personal public relations—to make yourself known as a polished professional. You can wait to be called on, or you can volunteer to participate in seminars, panels, conventions, conferences, and sales presentations.

Using the strategies in this chapter can help you "go for it" now with confidence. Just remember that Proper Preparation and Practice Prevent Poor Performance.

CUSTOMIZING TRAINING

Getting Your Needs Met Outside and Inside Your Organization

9

One Creative Training Technique is to make the best use of your resources. When you don't have all the necessary resources available within your own organization, you have to look elsewhere—outside your organization. Fortunately, there are lots of resources out there. Consultants who can work with you to create what you need. College professors who are experts in specific subjects. Larger consulting companies that have experienced staffs. And training companies that have off-the-shelf programs suitable for your needs.

EXPLORING OUTSIDE OPTIONS

Here are some key questions you should ask before you decide to select and work with an outside resource.

1. How Are the Training Objectives Generated?

Do the objectives come from you? Are they generated by a needs assessment done by you or by the outside resource you're considering working with on this project? Or—watch out here—are they generated from the prepackaged training program "that will surely meet all your needs"?

Training must be designed to get results and solve problems. One test you can use with consultants from the outside is to ask what objectives they would have for the program you have in mind. Ideally, their response should indicate a willingness and an ability to focus on what you need, not on what they have available.

2. For Whom Have They Worked?

Anyone you use should be able to provide references. I once did a consulting project for a large casino/hotel in Atlantic City. During my initial phone discussion with the client's training director, she asked for the names of three other clients of mine whom she could contact. About an hour after our conversation, I called each of those clients as a courtesy, simply to let them know that they might be contacted. Each had already talked with the training director and answered the following questions.

- What's the largest group Bob Pike has worked with for you?
- What's the smallest group?
- What's the biggest problem you've seen him handle with a group?
- When are you planning to use him next?

Good questions, aren't they? You might take a tip from this training director: Get the references when you're in a position to contact them immediately, *before* the consultant under consideration can. Also, once you've asked for three references, ask for three more. Then contact the second three. Almost anyone who's been around for a while can give you three strong references. But you may learn more that will be useful to you from the second three.

3. Why Should I Hire You?

A very direct question. And one that should provide you with some interesting answers that can help you compare your options.

4. Will There Be Pilot Programs?

Generally, I believe the answer to this question should be yes. Even a program that's been used off-the-shelf with large numbers of people probably should be considered a pilot program the first time it's offered to your group.

5. How Will the Pilot Program Be Structured?

A good pilot program will consist of a cross section of the target audience to be trained. In other words, there should be some marginal performers, some who fall in the middle, and some who are outstanding. The idea is to see how the program will work for your organization. The pilot should reflect, as much as possible, the make-up of a typical class. One modification you might want to make is to have some "senders" in attendance. What people are going to support and reinforce the training once it has been delivered? You may get better support if those individuals understand what kind of training their people will receive, and this understanding will be enhanced if they are present. If this isn't appropriate, consider scheduling an "executive briefing." This can be anything from a one-hour meeting at which the proposed course is described to an actual presentation of a mini-version of the course. The purpose is the same: to inform and gain the support of those whose subordinates will participate.

6. Who Will Do the Work?

Sometimes, larger organizations will have a lead consultant, whose name and credentials impress you, but the actual work may be done by others not as qualified. You have a right to know exactly who is going to perform the work. Who will be involved in the presentation? What is their track record? What are their credentials? Check this information carefully. Know what you're paying for.

The same is true of the contract you execute. Does it specify the people involved as well as the work to be performed? Make sure it does. You are, after all, buying people's time and expertise, so be an informed consumer.

7. Is This a "Turnkey" Program?

In other words, when the work is done, will you have everything you need to keep the program running in-house, if that's what you need or want? Are you buying the rights to *use* the materials—necessary instructor guides, visual aids, participant handouts—that are an integral part of the program? Or do you *own* the materials? Is the program designed in such a way that you, or others in your organization, can run it? Or will you always have to rely on someone from the outside? There's no right answer to any of these questions, but you should know what those answers are. It may cost more if you want to own the materials than simply use them, but that might be your choice. You might want a higher level of delivery than you can provide from within your organization; again, that's okay, as long as it's your choice.

8. Who Else Can Use the Material?

Is it important to restrict access of what's been developed? Would it hurt you if your competition had access to the same training materials? Is anything that's been used in the program proprietary? If so, have you protected yourself against unwanted disclosure?

9. Are You Listening or Talking?

Again, I don't think there's a right or wrong answer to this question, but do consider it. Do you want someone who's asking you the right questions? Or someone who's spending time sharing credentials, past accomplishments, etc.? Is the person willing or, better yet, eager to listen to your needs, your problems, the approaches you think might work? Or does the consultant have the solution before you've laid out the problem?

10. How Quickly Can the Consultant Provide an Answer?

Nobody knows everything. Beware the person who has an instant answer for every question. The best and brightest consultants ought to be stumped occasionally and have to dig a little before giving a response.

11. Does the Consultant Offer to Do a Needs Analysis?

Or does he or she at least want to know about what other approaches you've taken and when? Things change over time. You want to be sure that you're solving the right problem with the right methods. Only a complete and thorough needs analysis can help assure that you're on track. You may not be in a position to do an extensive analysis, but the consultant should at least offer to assess your needs.

Several years ago, I was asked to design a curriculum for a department of a large utility. The process would be used at the same time to train the trainers within the department to continue to use the steps to develop future courses as the need arose. I asked about a needs assessment and was told that a very complete one had been done 18 months earlier. I suggested that we schedule a few focus groups to validate the data from the earlier assessment, as well as to increase buy-in for the new training as it was brought on-line. The focus groups revealed entirely different needs that were, in management's opinion, far more pressing. Therefore, the focus of the project changed, and the organization derived greater benefit. Never underestimate the power of a good front-end analysis.

12. How Complete Is the Proposal?

A good proposal should do more than just describe the end product and the cost. Does it show the development steps? Does it include time lines? Are there benchmarks or milestones that you'll be able to use along the way to measure progress and insure that you're on track? A complete and thorough proposal allows you to assess the kind of end product you're going to get by working with the person or firm you select. Be wary of the one-to-two-page proposal that hits the highlights but offers no substance.

SELECTING/MODIFYING/CUSTOMIZING OFF-THE-SHELF PROGRAMS

Before you select a prepackaged program, consider evaluating all program options by asking the following questions.

1. What Are the Program's Stated Goals?

Are they consistent with the needs you've identified? Does the program do more than you need? Does it do less and, therefore, require supplementation? Is the program a good "fit," or will it require so much alteration that you'd be better off building from scratch?

2. What About Program Design?

Is the design of the program suitable for your organization? Your culture? Your bias as a trainer? Is it instructor-led but participant-centered? Does it allow for participation? Is there plenty of "real-world" application built into the design? Does it take into account the experiences that your participants will bring to the program? Does it overlap with other programs you may already have in place? Will that overlap, if it exists, be viewed critically by others? Can the program be delivered in a variety of formats (e.g., multiple days, daily sessions, weekly sessions), or are you limited to one format? How many participants can the format accommodate? Can it be effective with more? With less? How much expertise is required by the presenter?

3. What About Program Pacing?

Does the program offer a variety of activities? Or are the same few repeated over and over again? Does it allow for more involvement and participation later in the day to increase the energy level of the participants? Is the pacing flexible? Can you slow down if the group is stuck on something? Can you speed up if everyone has grasped a concept? Are there alternative activities in case something that's been planned doesn't work and another approach is required to help drive home the point?

4. Is the Time Available Used Effectively?

Is there an appropriate blend of theory and application? Is there a good balance between presentation and application? Is the time spent on each topic area too long, too short, or just about right? Are the topics introduced in the proper sequence? Is class time used for things that could be referenced? Does the bulk of in-class time focus on what participants need to know and be able to do rather than on things they can find on their own? Do participants become sufficiently familiar with other resources (such as subject-matter experts, manuals, software, videotape, videodisk, etc.) available to them after the course is over? Can they access these resources, and are they comfortable in accessing them?

5. What's the Back-up Plan?

Assuming the first course is a pilot program, what's the back-up plan? If the scheduled instructor isn't available for some reason, who's the alternate? (Don't assume that an alternate isn't needed. Remember Murphy's Law—"Whatever can go wrong will." If the instructor hasn't missed an assignment in 20 years, perhaps he or she is about due to miss one.) Are materials to be shipped in advance? Make sure there's a cushion in the delivery date. Are you being given masters to reproduce? Put a cushion in the date when you're to receive them to insure proper reproduction. Ordering binders or other materials? Be sure to add a time cushion. Make sure there's a back-up plan for every key element.

6. Will the Program Be Viewed as Relevant by the Participants? By the Senders? By the Payers?

Can each of these three groups see the value of the content from their unique perspectives? Is the content relevant? Do the illustrations fit? Can participants readily make the transfer from the classroom to their work situations? Does the content address the most pressing business needs of the target audience from the perspective of each of these groups?

7. Does the Program Use Familiar Terminology?

For example, if you're considering using an off-the-shelf management-training program, is the terminology used consistent with the terminology the participants already know? If your organization refers to personal styles as dominant, influencing, supportive, and competent, is it worth it to introduce new terms that may describe the same things, such as driver, expressive, amiable, and analytical? Does the program use terms consistent with your industry?

Do the examples fit? In a selling course, are the examples all big-ticket, long-term sales even though your salespeople sell items that are short-term, one-call close? Are the examples consumer-oriented when your people are manufacturing-oriented? These differences can dilute the effectiveness of an otherwise good program.

8. What Logistics Are Required?

You may have selected a bargain program only to find that it requires small-group breakouts that necessitate expensive off-site arrangements. Overall, you no longer have a bargain. Or perhaps the design requires at least two instructors, but you can't spare two for a single course. Or the design depends upon small-group video feedback that requires three cameras, three videocassette recorders, three monitors, etc., and you own only one of each. Renting or purchasing the additional units may be possible, but it's an additional cost to consider. Make sure you check all the requirements and the *costs* for all the requirements before you make a decision.

TEN STEPS TO A PROGRAM THAT MEETS YOUR NEEDS

Whether you're working with an outside consultant to modify or build a training program or working with inside subject-matter experts (SMEs) to meet needs, here's a process that can help insure that your program is effective.

Step 1. Mind Mapping

One of the most effective program-development tools I have ever acquired is the mind map. I was first introduced to the concept when I took a speed reading course in the late '60s. In the course, we called it structured recall, and I've heard it referred to by other names, such as branching and spidergrams, but the concept is essentially the same. It worked so well that I continued to use it for several years to structure letters, memos, and papers and to facilitate notetaking during presentations I attended and as I read professional materials.

A tremendous amount has been written about the mind and how it works—right brain versus left brain, linear versus spatial, ad infinitum. My own theory is that most of us have minds like pinball machines: they don't generate thoughts in a linear pattern, but each thought generates two or three spin-off thoughts, rather like the steel ball bouncing around in a pinball machine. When we play pinball, we exercise some control, but the arrangement of the inner pattern of the machine significantly affects where the ball goes.

The human brain contains over one trillion brain cells called neurons. Each neuron is capable of interconnecting with the neurons that surround it in hundreds of ways. Every time we have a thought, it fires a synapse (the connector between neurons) and creates a chain reaction. This makes possible new connections and relationships we might never have logically foreseen.

Mind mapping allows us to see spatially how concepts and information might relate in ways that standard notetaking or outlining don't allow.

Here's one mind map (recreated using a Macintosh® and MacDraw© and MacPaint© software) I created in ten minutes for a Creative Training Techniques seminar.

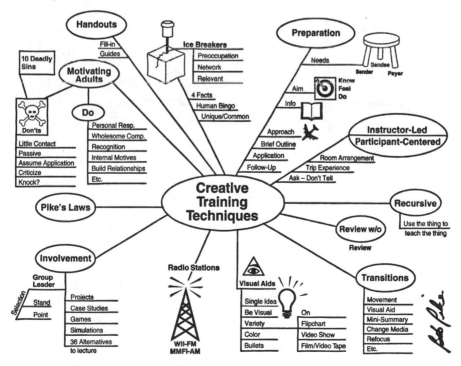

Here are some fundamentals of mind mapping.
- It's free flowing.
- Don't worry about where anything goes for now.
- Use only key words.
- It's your tool; let it work for you.
- Feel free to connect things that relate.
- Feel free to go back and add.
- Try short bursts. Time yourself for five minutes, take a two-minute break, then spend five minutes adding, adjusting, etc.

Mind mapping can be done alone or with groups. Here's a mind map of a Creative Training Techniques seminar that a group produced in 20 minutes to summarize the seminar.

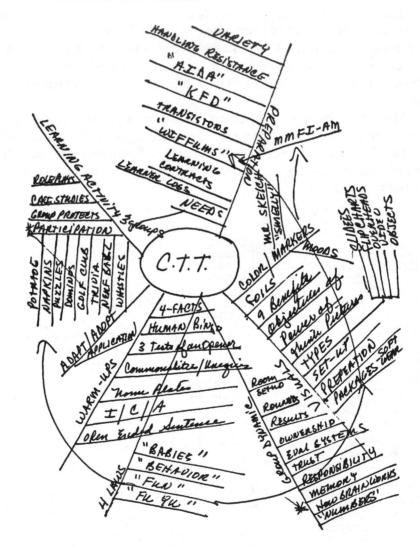

In 1985, I was working with a large computer company to modify some of its technical courses. The model I provided the trainers with whom I was working is the one we're using in this chapter. We started by taping together several large sheets of flip-chart paper and mounting them on the wall where everyone could see what was happening. We determined the core concepts of the course and placed them on the mind map. Then we took the input of the subject-matter experts (SMEs) and added it to the mind map. We continued until we had a thorough picture of the course content.

As you may know, SMEs tend to give you all the information that anyone in the world could ever want about their subject. But the participants of your training program may not need that amount of information or level of expertise. This dilemma leads to Step Two.

Step 2. Minimalist Sets

In any training program, you're likely to have the "need to know" and the "nice to know" and the "never need to know."

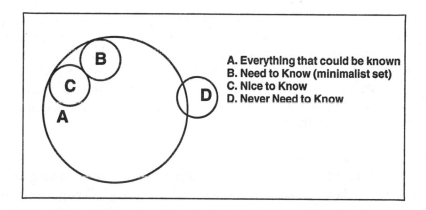

A. Everything that could be known
B. Need to Know (minimalist set)
C. Nice to Know
D. Never Need to Know

A subject-matter expert or a group of SMEs may generate a content list or competency list so long that the SMEs themselves would be challenged to accomplish it. The question we're asking here is: What's the *least* somebody in the course would need to know or be able to do in order for the course to be considered successful for that person? This step may involve several things. Such as asking those for whom a training program is being designed what's needed in the program. It may involve asking the supervisors of those individuals. It may involve asking the people one level below them. For the program to have the necessary level of support, we need the input of the senders, those sent, and the payers. We want agreement up front of what success will look like. This enables us to pare down the content that we had on our mind map. It also enables us to proceed to Step Three.

Step 3. Choose Order/Methods

What sequence are we going to use in covering the course content? Our choices include these:

- General to specific
- Simple to complex
- Most important to least important
- Primary to secondary
- Whole to parts

These different sequence patterns may all be effective in various parts of the same course.

Step 4. Brainstorm Approaches

What are all the possible approaches to delivering the course? If participants have information or experience relevant to the content, then discovery methods such as group discussion, brainstorming, games, or simulations can be used. But if participants lack knowledge or experience, then methods such as lecture, symposium, or panel discussions may be more suitable.

Another consideration concerns the time of day each segment will be presented. This is the nitty-gritty. If the course lasts for a day, what do we do to energize people in the afternoon? What parts of our content do people need to master? What should they need to be able to find when they need it? For each part of the program, what are two or three alternative delivery methods? How do we maintain variety, not using any method too frequently or for too long at any one time?

Step 5. Rehearse Individual Modules

Each part is practiced by itself. Does each component have a strong opening and close? Is the middle supported and reinforced? Components that are introduced just before or after program breaks should be especially strong and engaging.

Step 6. Test New Material

Whenever you include totally new material in a program, be sure to test it. If it's printed instructions, give them to several people beforehand to be sure they can follow the instructions. If you have new visual aids, be sure they communicate clearly the concepts you intend. If you're adding material, ask what, if anything, you should delete to make room for these additions.

Step 7. Dry Run of Program

This dry run will vary, based on the time and money available and the significance of the program. I've had dry runs of a three-day program that were as short as half a day; I simply "walked through" the components because I was familiar with them, but perhaps the sequence was new, or I had made slight alterations I wanted to check. For one major program I helped develop, we had a one-week dry run of a two-week program. The five faculty members were on-site, along with the ten members of the company's advisory committee for the program. We presented to the advisory committee exactly what we planned to do each minute of each day. Some parts we talked through, some parts we walked through, and some parts we ran through. We described how all the assignments would be made, how groups would be formed, etc. The advisory group thoroughly evaluated each part of the program from the organization's perspective. Three weeks later, after lots of revisions, we did the pilot program, which lasted a full two weeks.

Step 8. Pilot Program

This is the real thing. It's a full program, just like every other program you'll run; but since it's the first, you won't be able to make all the adjustments that are needed for the program to work as well as possible. Make sure the participants evaluate the program *after it's over*, not at each step along the way. If you're continually stopping to discuss each component, neither you nor they will ever get a feel for the program flow.

Step 9. Evaluate Program

Get all the feedback you can from all the interested parties you can. This may include the senders, those sent, and the payers. You want your program to be as good as you can make it.

There are a number of things you may want people to evaluate:

1. The facilities
2. The level at which the content was developed
3. The instructor's knowledge of the subject
4. The instructor's interest in the participants
5. The usefulness of the content
6. The usefulness of the handouts
7. The effectiveness of the visual aids
8. The applicability of the content back on the job
9. The length of time spent on each topic (too long, too short, just about right)
10. What helped the course be effective?
11. What hindered the course's effectiveness?
12. What would you want to change?

When you develop an evaluation form, be sure that you consider three different types of feedback items on the form. Number one is to use a numerical rating or Likert scale. For example you could use a seven point scale with seven being the highest. But secondly, also allow open-ended questions. Allow people to describe for you why they gave the various ratings that they did. And thirdly, consider multiple-choice ratings.

Here's an example from one of our seminars. The content area is preparation, and we allow people to indicate on a scale from one to seven how valuable that information was, from "Very Useful" on number seven to "Not Useful" on number one. But notice that there are only three options that we can use:

Was the amount of material covered:

a. too long

b. too short

c. just about right

Was the pace of the material too long, too short, just about right? Was the level that the material was presented at too low, too high, just about right? This feedback can be useful in improving future offerings of the course.

APPLICATIONS FOR CREATIVE TRAINERS
FEEDBACK/EVALUATION - MINNEAPOLIS 12/6-7/93

We want to make our future sessions and communications as meaningful as possible and we would appreciate your candid evaluation of this program in response to the questions below. Please leave this form with the seminar leader before you depart.

Please PRINT your name and address below for mailing.

Name_____Title_____
Organization_____
Business Address_____
City_____State_____Zip Code_____
Telephone (   )_____

Section Evaluation:

		Very Useful	Somewhat Useful	Not Useful		Amount of Time Spent Too Long (TL), Too Short (TS), or Just About Right (JAR)	
I.	General Concepts of Human Behavior	7 6 5 4 3 2 1			TL	TS	JAR
II.	Visuals in Training	7 6 5 4 3 2 1			TL	TS	JAR
III.	Interactive Learning Activities	7 6 5 4 3 2 1			TL	TS	JAR
IV.	Assessment Instruments	7 6 5 4 3 2 1			TL	TS	JAR
V.	Skill Surveys	7 6 5 4 3 2 1			TL	TS	JAR
VI.	Videos in Training	7 6 5 4 3 2 1			TL	TS	JAR
VII.	Skill Practice/Role Plays	7 6 5 4 3 2 1			TL	TS	JAR
VIII.	Make or Buy Decision	7 6 5 4 3 2 1			TL	TS	JAR

On a scale of 1 to 7 - with 7 being the highest - how would you rate the following:

	High						Low
Overall Course	7	6	5	4	3	2	1
Instructors Knowledge of Content	7	6	5	4	3	2	1
Instructors Interest in Audience	7	6	5	4	3	2	1
Instructors Style of Training	7	6	5	4	3	2	1
Usefulness of Program Materials	7	6	5	4	3	2	1
Effectiveness of Visual Aids	7	6	5	4	3	2	1

What did you like most about the program?
_____
_____
_____
_____

What would you like to see changed for future programs?
_____
_____
_____
_____

Step 10. Adjust Program

Based on the feedback you get, recycle all the steps we've just been through to modify, adjust, and adapt to fit the needs of your group.

CLOSING THE CIRCLE

10

Putting It All Together:
Some Final Thoughts

In this final chapter, I'd like to share with you some practical tips and guidelines that I think can be of use to anyone who considers himself or herself a training professional. Let's start with the seven laws of learning.

APPLYING THE SEVEN LAWS OF LEARNING TO YOUR PRESENTATION

1. The Law of the TEACHER

The teacher must know what is to be taught. You can't teach what you haven't learned. And you must teach from a prepared life, as well as from a prepared lesson. The most effective instructors on any topic generally are those who have experienced what they are teaching.

There are two types of knowledge: intellectual knowledge and experiential knowledge. People like learning not from people who simply talk about a subject but from people who have lived the subject. They want to learn from those who have not only head knowledge but also heart knowledge. Have you paid—or are you paying—the price to know from experience what you share with your participants? That's the only way you'll be able to stand before others and have absolute confidence in what you're saying. That's the only way you'll know, in whatever learning situation you find yourself, that you won't be "scraping the bottom of the barrel" in communicating with your group. Remember the words of C.S. Lewis, the English philosopher: "A man with an experience is never at the mercy of a man with an argument." There's a power that goes into the classroom with you when you know what you know not simply through the head but through the heart—from solid, practical experience.

2. The Law of the LEARNER

The learner must attend with interest to the material being presented. If you're excited about what you're teaching, you can create a motivational environment. You can do that by answering the learner's question: "What's in it for me?" The learner has to see the benefits for himself or herself.

What will they get out of it? How can they apply it? How can they use it?

The saying "You can lead a horse to water, but you can't make him drink" is true, but it's just as true that you can salt the oats. When people see how they'll benefit from the training personally, they'll be attentive. And they'll learn more than you and I probably think they're capable of learning—and in a shorter period of time. Don't ever underestimate the power of desire. Or the power of belief. When people believe in themselves and in the goals they've set, they can accomplish more than we can imagine.

3. The Law of the LANGUAGE
The language you use must be comprehensible to the learner. Nobody likes experts; we want to knock them off their pedestals. But everybody loves the learner. Start where people are, and take them where they need to be. Go from the known to the unknown. When you use new words or terms unfamiliar to the learners, define them immediately. Language should be a stepping stone, not a stumbling block.

4. The Law of the LESSON
The truth or content to be taught must be learned through the truth or the content that is already known. Again, go from where the learners are. Build on what they already know.

I once attended a seminar that dealt with some new concepts pertaining to the psychology of personality. Since I have an academic background in psychology and counseling, I was really interested in what the speaker had to say. She began her presentation by saying, "In order to really understand what I'm about to say, you have to be willing to forget everything you've ever learned about personality and everything that you've ever learned about Freud, Jung, Adler, Maslow, MacGregor, and Rogers. Because if you think about their concepts of personality, you'll have difficulty grasping this one. When I first looked at it, I couldn't understand it myself. Only after nine or ten months of struggling with these new ideas could I finally see how they worked and why."

Do you know how difficult it is to not think about things you already know? The almost universal consensus of the group at the end of the 90-minute presentation was that it was literally impossible to set aside what we knew and forget about it so that we could learn some new concepts that might conflict with the old. And that was based on the feelings of the 40 or so of those who were left from a group of over 200 at the beginning of the presentation! The rest couldn't even make it to the end.

Perhaps the speaker in question should have said, "As I have examined various models or concepts of personality and the psychology of personality, I have found many of them helpful. But parts of them cause me problems. For example…" Then she briefly could have reviewed the theories of personality, saying, for example, "Freud has these things to say about personality… And Jung believed…" She could have repeated this process for the other personality theorists and then said, "That's why I'm interested in these new ideas that I'll present to you today. While they may seem very, very different, I think you'll see how they answer those problems I have raised, the problems I had in reviewing these other concepts of personality." This approach would have acknowledged the benefits that can be gained from our prior knowledge and, at the same time, made us aware of potential problems. It would have prepared us to be receptive to new knowledge.

5. The Law of the TEACHING PROCESS

You must excite and direct your learners' self-motivation. People often learn best through self-discovery. I've frequently said that there are basically three ways people learn, and two of them don't work, so we don't use them.

1. You can tell people things. For example, you can stand up in front of a group and say, "The first thing you need to understand is that you're all lousy listeners. Now that I've told you that, let me give you some tips for effective listening." Ideally, members of your audience will think, "Boy, I really appreciate your pointing out what my problem is. How can I improve?" Now, that would be nice, but it's more likely that they'll think, "I am *not* a lousy listener. You're a lousy talker. If you had something interesting to say, I'd listen. But you don't, so I won't. It's your problem that I'm not listening, not my problem."

2. You can use statistics. For example, you can say something like, "According to all the latest behavioral studies, 95 percent of all people are lousy listeners." The unfortunate part of something like this is that frequently you'll get a room full of people together and they'll say, "You know, you're absolutely right. What can we do to help them? I wish my boss was here. I wish my spouse was here. I wish my employees were here." This is because we tend to have a "not me" syndrome.

3. We can put people in situations where they discover for themselves how effective or ineffective they are. People learn most effectively when they are actively involved in the learning process, not passively observing it.

6. The Law of the LEARNING PROCESS

The learner must reproduce in his or her own life the content to be learned. Learning does not take place until behavior has changed. We're talking about being able to apply—not simply to know but also to do. Just because the instructor has rapport with the learners doesn't automatically guarantee that learning is going to occur. You want to involve as many senses as possible and use as many approaches as you can so that people grasp and apply the material you want them to learn.

7. *The Law of REVIEW and APPLICATION*

You must confirm the completion of the content taught. And you do that by emphasizing practical application. Ask, "How can you use this in real life?" and "What do you expect if you apply what you've been learning?"

These are the seven laws of learning that, as you review and apply them, can help you be a more effective trainer. Number one says, "Do you, as the instructor or presenter, have personal experience in applying what you're about to teach?" Number two says, "Throughout your presentation, do you constantly emphasize for the participants the answer to 'What's in it for me?'" Number three says, "Do you always speak so that the participants can understand? Do you ever practice one-upmanship?" Number four says, "Are you willing to go from the known to the unknown? Do you start from where they are, establish a base line that they can then build from?" Number five says, "Do you get people involved?" Number six says, "Learning does not take place until behavior is changed. It is not simply a matter of showing that you can do it but of demonstrating to them that *they* can do it." And finally, number seven says, "Do you show people how to apply it in real life?"

THE 22 DEADLY SINS...

That Cause People to Walk Out, Ask for Their Money Back, Send Letters of Complaint, and in Other Ways Torpedo Your Speaking, Presenting, and Training Efforts

1. *Appearing Unprepared*

This does not mean that you actually *are* unprepared; it simply means that you *seem* to be. Examples of an appearance of unpreparedness would be not being able to locate your next transparency or not knowing what comes next unless you have your notes right in front of you. A presenter who appears unprepared runs the risk of appearing unqualified to be presenting.

2. *Starting Late*

Whether everyone is there or not, start on time. Otherwise, we penalize those who are on time and reward those who are late. Be on time yourself. And on time for the instructor means early. My rule of thumb is that, in a facility I control, I'm there an hour before starting time to check the setup, materials, etc. In a facility I don't control, it's two to three hours ahead of time, depending upon the complexity of the setup. Thirty minutes before the seminar is not the time to find that the room has been incorrectly arranged or the necessary equipment hasn't arrived or doesn't work. Another rule of thumb: The last 15 minutes before class starts is for interaction with the participants.

3. Handling Questions Improperly

This means putting off questions, perhaps abruptly, by saying something like "I'll be covering that in a little while. Please wait until then." Or combining questions and deciding to give one answer to two slightly different questions: "Those two questions are somewhat similar, so I'll just answer them together." Or giving people the impression that theirs is an awkward question, a dumb question, or a question that didn't need to be asked. All these are examples of improper handling of questions.

4. Apologizing for Yourself or the Organization

If there's a problem, in all likelihood 80 percent of your participants won't be aware of it. Take care of the people for whom there is a problem on an individual basis.

Recently, I attended a conference of about 600 people. The conference chairman came to the platform at the beginning of a general session and said, "I know that some of you had a problem with cockroaches in your rooms last night. The exterminators are spraying your rooms, and I've been assured by the hotel that you won't have any further problems." Later, I found out that the problem actually had affected only three people. But how many do you think were affected after they heard the chairman's announcement?

5. Being Unfamiliar with Knowable Information

For example, not knowing the names of the key executives who are sitting in on an executive briefing or not knowing the name of the organization to which you're making a presentation. I once heard someone say, "I really appreciated being invited to make this presentation to the American Society for Training Directors;" in fact, he was addressing the American Society for Training and Development. Know that an organization has clients, not customers, or patients rather than clients and that a company has associates, which are never referred to as employees.

6. Using Audio Visuals Unprofessionally

This includes things like not knowing how to operate the slide projector or showing poorly prepared transparencies. As audiences become increasingly sophisticated, they expect not only to be able to read any visuals used but also that those visuals are interesting enhancements to your presentation.

7. Seeming to be Off Schedule

In your introduction, you may have indicated that you are going to cover ten things in a one-day presentation. By lunch, you've covered two of them. Now, in your own mind you know that's exactly where you're supposed to be because those two points provide the major base for the other eight that you'll introduce in the remaining time. But unless you explain that timeframe, your audience will assume that five points should have been covered before lunch and five after. As far as they're concerned, you're way behind, and you're probably going to cram a lot of information into the afternoon session.

In order not to appear off schedule, tell participants where you're going and how long it's going to take to get there.

8. Not Involving the Participants

The more you can involve people in the learning process, the more effective that learning is going to be. Adults bring experiences and expertise to your presentations, and they want those contributions acknowledged. In a presupervisory training course, you may have people who have never supervised; but they've *been* supervised, so they understand the distinctions between good and bad supervision. New salespeople have never sold, but they've been customers, so they know what it's like to be on the other side of the table. Take advantage of what the participants bring to the program.

9. Not Establishing Personal Rapport

Simple ways to develop personal rapport are: making and maintaining eye contact throughout your presentation and simply being available to your participants at breaks, at lunch, and before and after sessions. Always try to be available 15 minutes before the start of a presentation, 15 minutes after the end of a presentation, and for at least half of any scheduled break.

10. Ending Late

This is even worse than starting late. I've never yet known a group that was pleased when a training program or presentation ran over the scheduled time. A guideline I use is to begin tying things together 15 minutes before the end of an hour presentation, 30 minutes before the end of a three-hour presentation, and 45 minutes before the end of a six-hour presentation. That way I not only finish on schedule but I have time for a solid wrap-up that gives a sense of closure to the process.

11. Appearing Disorganized

You appear disorganized when you don't properly introduce things, you don't provide logical transitions from one part of your presentation to the next, and/or you don't summarize what you've been talking about. Remember: Tell them what you're going to tell them, and then tell them what you've told them.

12. Not Quickly Establishing a Positive Image

At the beginning of most presentations, people need some time to get focused, to get themselves going. But that's difficult if the person making the presentation also needs to take time to get focused and get going. Get started quickly by introducing a vivid illustration and by involving the group by asking questions. If you quickly take command, you give people the impression that you know who you are, where you are, and where you're going and that it is going to be exciting and fun for them to come along.

Actually, you establish an image of yourself and your program even before you open your mouth—by the way people were prepared to come to the program, by the look and feel of the materials that informed them of the program, by the handouts and manuals they received as they registered, by the type of facility in which the program is conducted, and by how you, as the instructor, are dressed.

I believe we ought to dress just a little more formally than our participants expect. It's better to be a bit overdressed and make ourselves more casual by removing a jacket, loosening a tie, rolling up sleeves, etc., than to be the most casually attired person in the room. We show participants respect by the way we dress.

13. Not Covering the Objectives Promised

In every class, there will be someone who checks very carefully to see that everything that has been promised has been delivered. Joel Weldon, a Phoenix-based consultant, makes this suggestion: "Promise much, deliver more." I agree. First, though, we must make sure that we deliver what we promised—and then give the value-added material, the unexpected extras that can boost the program's success.

14. Not Scheduling Enough Breaks

Everybody may not be as fascinated with the subject as we are. But even the most interested participant can only concentrate for so long. We need to let people stretch and move around. Consider giving participants at least ten minutes of break for every hour in the classroom. These mini-breaks allow for some stretching and walking activities and are in addition to the standard refreshment breaks.

15. Practicing Bad Habits

Check this one by videotaping yourself periodically to pick up on bad habits that may have crept into your presentation style. If you find that you absentmindedly jingle change, take the change out of your pocket. If you lean on the lectern as you present, move away from the lectern. Keep your hands in your pockets too much? Hold onto something. Do you punctuate your delivery with non-words, such as "um" or "er"? Practice should help eliminate these verbal ticks.

Getting rid of distracting habits and mannerisms can enhance the effectiveness of our presentations.

16. Not Checking the Environment

Avoid this by diligently checking—and checking yet again—all elements of the presentation setting: room setup, temperature, light, sound, equipment, and all materials you'll use yourself and distribute to participants.

17. Not Updating Material

Participants expect us to be current, and we should be. As professionals, we can't become complacent with either our presentation style or content. When was the last time you revised your written materials, visuals, etc.?

18. Not Admitting Mistakes

As presenters, we're not perfect; we make mistakes, and we don't have all the answers. When we don't know an answer or we do make a mistake, we must admit it, either to an individual or, if appropriate, to the entire group.

19. Using Inappropriate Humor

Any humor that offends or makes fun of any participant is inappropriate and will kill your presentation. Generally speaking, it's best to avoid humor that relates to sex, politics, or religion.

20. Using Inappropriate Language

I once sat in on a presentation made by a friend of mine who had a national reputation in his field. He spent the first ten minutes explaining that some of the language he would use was just for effect and that no one who had attended his previous presentations had ever been offended once they understood that. He proceeded with his presentation, which was peppered with the raw language he had referred to. The person next to me remarked, "I don't care if no one else has ever been offended, *I* am!"

A nationally known consultant has made a set of best-selling videotapes that a client of mine refused to purchase until the speaker granted permission for the client to "bleep" certain words he felt would be offensive to some members of the company's work force.

I offer these two examples to emphasize the power of language. Tasteless words and phrases can taint an otherwise satisfactory presentation.

21. Coming on As an Expert, a Know-it-all

Most of us *are* experts at what we do, which is training, and that's why the training responsibility falls on our shoulders. But that expertise shouldn't be flaunted to the point that it makes participants fell small. We can demonstrate our expertise without belittling others. Our advanced knowledge hardly makes us superior human beings.

22. Using Poor Grammar, Pronunciation, and Enunciation

Don't let participants think, "*How* you say it sounds so awful that I can't hear *what* you say." Once again, get out the video camera. Each of us can improve our verbal delivery skills; there's a little of George Bernard Shaw's Eliza Doolittle in all of us.

USING YOUR OWN PERSONAL EXPERIENCES

Feel free, when you deliver training presentations, to use your personal experiences. Participants can readily identify with the triumphs and the mistakes that you relate. And this identification helps establish a common ground, an invaluable personal rapport. In a very subtle way, it also helps solidify your authority as an instructor. As you share personal illustrations of how you've applied this content and made it work for you, you demonstrate to the participants that they will be able to do the same. Be sure that your illustrations are balanced between trials and triumphs; don't discourage participants by talking only about how you have *always* succeeded in your professional endeavors. Unless you are an absolutely perfect person, show people that you are human and that you've learned not only from your triumphs but also from your mistakes.

WHY HANDOUTS CAN BE ALMOST AS IMPORTANT AS THE PRESENTATION ITSELF

Throughout this book, I've emphasized the need for application. One involvement technique that I've alluded to several times is that of giving people handouts for them to complete. Two examples are partial transparencies on which they fill in key words and partial outlines that they complete as the session proceeds. This activity keeps participants involved in the learning process and also gives them something of value that they can refer to in the future.

This simple involvement technique also allows you to cover more material in less time. A well-prepared handout indicates in a nonverbal way that you're thoroughly and thoughtfully prepared for the presentation. It tells your participants that you cared enough about this presentation to prepare superior supplemental materials.

THE SEMINAR WORKBOOK: A CHECKLIST OF IDEAS

The seminar workbook usually is not designed to stand alone; it is a support to the seminar, a supplement. It may contain materials to be used in the seminar, as well as resources to be consulted after the program is over. If you do include material for use both during and after the seminar, consider printing the materials on two different-colored papers. This keeps participants from being overwhelmed by the amount of material they may be receiving, and it also keeps them from thinking you're behind in the program because you haven't covered all the material in the manual.

Here is a checklist of methods and materials you can use to make your handouts, your presentations, and your seminars more complete and more effective.

1. Topics that will be covered in various sections of the program.
2. A checklist that attendees can actually use on their jobs. This can be a sequence of steps to take in a process, items needed to perform a task, elements to include in a project.
3. A list of points that will be fully or partially covered, but that would require extensive note keeping to record in full.
4. Schematics of a technical process.
5. A systems flow chart.
6. Reprints of articles (including those by the seminar leader).
7. A summary of key points. (This material would typically be projected on an overhead as well.)
8. A humorous perspective on the topic.
9. A bibliography.
10. Formulas. (This material should be projected.)
11. Graphs (projected).
12. Photographs (projected).
13. Definitions that the seminar leader will discuss but that are time-consuming to write down.
14. Section dividers. (Divide your workbook into modular sections.)
15. Sample correspondence.
16. Case studies.

CONCLUSION

We've reached the end of the cafeteria line for now. At the beginning, I said I would offer you a smorgasbord of ideas that are practical, reasonable, and effective. A cafeteria approach allows you to go through the line and take what you can use. I hope that your meal has been satisfying, and I hope you'll try some of these ideas, which have worked well for me and for many others. If you've got some new twists that you'd like to share, let me hear from you. There's always room for each of us to grow and improve.

I hope that you continue to become more effective and have a greater impact on those around you because of these ideas.

Finally, I hope you realize that, although this is the end of the book, it may be the beginning of some new and rewarding professional experiences for you and those who participate in your training endeavors.

APPENDIX 1

Potpourri

In preparing *The Creative Training Techniques Handbook*, I came across a couple of lists that I had written for seminar participants. The content of each list seems relevant to the content of this book but doesn't fit naturally into any one chapter. I offer the following nuggets here for you to mine and use.

27 FACTORS THAT CAN MAKE OR BREAK A MEETING

1. Have a complete agenda.
2. Start and end on time.
3. Keep speakers' introductions brief.
4. Pay attention to small details. Use coffee cups instead of Styrofoam, glasses instead of disposable cups.
5. Provide a pad and pencil for each participant.
6. Use a coffee-break alternative. Distribute Popsicles instead!
7. Provide a nonalcoholic alternative at receptions.
8. Be prompt with a post-meeting follow-up.
9. Create opportunities for members to mix.
10. Serve lighter lunches and skip dessert. This helps participants remain alert all afternoon.
11. Allow adequate break time for renewing friendships and informal networking.
12. Make your preparation obvious to everyone. Have a check-in staff that is prepared and knowledgeable.
13. Use variety in your room setups. For example, for a two-day program, use banquet rounds on day one and herringbone 6′ x 30″ tables the next day.
14. Check out the audio system beforehand.
15. Make certain that meetings won't be interrupted. Tell the facility management that calls should be held, etc.
16. Know whom you should contact if there are problems with the facility—for example, the room is too hot or too cold.

17. Check out the facilities before the meeting begins to see that room setup and AV requirements have been met.

18. Make registration simple and easy.

19. If you have a two- or three-day meeting, offer a spouse program. Check out special happenings and points of interest in the city where you are meeting.

20. Make certain that program materials are shipped to a specific person at the meeting site; otherwise, they may be misplaced. Also, clearly mark them as 1 of 3, 2 of 3, etc., to avoid confusion.

21. Send a detailed cover letter along with your signed contract that explains exactly what you expect from the facility staff. Include a few facts about what you *don't* want to have happen.

22. Be available. If you are unable to be at your meeting, confirm with your speaker and facility contact that, should a problem arise, you are only a phone call away.

23. Send copies of facility agreements to all speakers and other necessary meeting staff.

24. If your meeting will last more than one day, arrive a day early. If it is a single-day meeting, arrive at least two hours beforehand.

25. Have your meeting place compatible with your objectives. For example, don't schedule meetings for 16 hours a day in a resort setting or for 4 hours a day where there are no activities available.

26. Have an agreement with your speakers about "selling" during his/her presentation. Nothing turns off an audience more than being subjected to unsolicited commercials.

27. Have your speakers available for informal discussions and functions immediately after presentations and during social hours and meals. Avoid "hit and run" presentations.

WAYS TO EVALUATE TRAINING

1. Ask: How does the training contribute to the organization's goals? Does your training solve "performance problems"? The problems to be solved must be identified and agreed upon in advance. Management must agree on what constitutes improvement before the training begins.

2. Ask: Does the training achieve learning objectives? In other words, what can the trainees do now or what do they know now that they couldn't do or didn't know before?

3. Ask: Does the training have perceived value? Do the trainees, their managers, and the people who provide the budget feel that the training is practical, relevant, and useful? You must decide whose opinions count and how they are expressed.

4. Identify the tasks the job requires, including under what conditions,

along with performance standards. Pre- and post-test participants on their ability to meet those standards.

5. Evaluate the effectiveness of instructors and others involved in delivering the training.

6. Evaluate the timeliness and frequency of opportunities to perform the new skills and behaviors back on the job.

7. Evaluate the timeliness, frequency, and appropriateness of on-the-job feedback and support.

8. Use the experimental approach. Compare trained versus untrained or pre- and post-trained participants or some combination of both.

9. Use the critical-incident approach. Collect specific incidents or stories that support how the training improved performance.

10. Use the problem-solving approach. Rather than offering "generic," one-size-fits-all training, design and deliver training geared to a specific, identified, agreed-upon problem.

11. Evaluate the program's opening. Did it get agreement of needs, state objectives, and establish learner accountability?

12. Evaluate the learning experiences. Were they "real-life"? Relevant? Involving? Did they provide learners with feedback?

13. Evaluate communication. Was the presentation clear to all learners? Did the nonverbal aspects support the verbal aspects?

14. Evaluate instructor attitudes. Were they inoffensive to all learners? Did they stimulate the interest of all learners?

15. Evaluate training objectives. To what extent did participants achieve the prespecified objectives?

16. Identify the strongest features of the training program.

17. Identify the weakest features of the training program.

18. Have participants list new ideas they picked up as a result of the program—or new behaviors they will practice.

19. Ask supervisors to answer the above question for their participants.

APPENDIX 2

Graphics

Graphics are becoming an increasingly important consideration in designing and delivering training. The widespread availability of personal computers to the training department, along with graphics packages that are relatively user-friendly, puts higher-quality graphics within almost everyone's reach.

In this appendix, I will briefly describe two things: software and hardware that I use and have used on a regular basis and other graphics packages that meet the following criteria:

- They are widely available.
- They support, at a minimum, plotters, dot matrix and laser printers as output devices.
- They provide, at a minimum, formats for horizontal and vertical bar charts, pie and exploded pie charts, and line and scatter charts.
- I have always used DOS-based computers; I have, by necessity, had to limit my comments to programs that are IBM-compatible.

WHAT I USE

I began using VideoShow and PictureIt when General Parametrics introduced them in 1984. VideoShow allows you to use a standard CGA (color graphics adapter) color monitor (which, incidentally, is the least-expensive monitor) and allows the presentation of 2000 x 500 resolution graphics with a choice of 1000 colors. When you consider that, most of the time, choices have been limited to 600 x 350 resolution and 4 colors of 16, you can appreciate the difference.

VideoShow is the hardware part of the system. Essentially, it's a computer the size of an attaché case that is easily portable, can be connected to almost any television, computer monitor, or video projector, and allows you to display, either in sequence or out of sequence, any of the images you have created.

The VideoShow HQ that I use today costs $4999 and weighs 8 pounds. The images I create can be displayed on a monitor (which is what I do most of the time) and can be output to slides or color transparencies or even printed out as hard copy for handouts on a laser or dot-matrix printer.

PictureIt is the primary software I use. It's extremely user-friendly. I could create a visual after about 45 minutes, the documentation was easy to follow, and after, about 8 to 10 hours, I was producing some pretty sophisticated visuals. The system allows me to build in automatically special effects such as wipes, fades, and dissolves as transitions between images. There are 28 predesigned formats for bar charts, line charts, pie charts, and word charts. Each format has its own default colors; if I don't choose, it's chosen for me. So if I'm in a hurry, I can get variety of colors just by varying the format I choose.

After getting comfortable with PictureIt, I added PicturePaks from Imageline. These are predesigned graphics libraries that allow me to select a very sophisticated image and simply add my text, combine the two, and produce a very polished product. Each PicturePak contains about 80 images. There are separate PicturePaks available for a variety of subjects. The images retail for $195.

The last bit of expertise I added was Freelance Plus. This package, now a Lotus Development Product, allowed me to add freeform graphics. This meant being able to create logos to customize my presentation for a client, etc.

Thanks to these packages, my visuals are consistently rated as outstanding wherever I've presented. All of us who conduct the Creative Training Techniques seminar have a VideoShow system, so we've made a commitment to this technology. While the initial expense has made some trainers gasp, in the long run it's been cost-effective because it lets us rapidly update visuals.

I like VideoShow for the following reasons:

- It's easy to use.
- It's portable.
- When I design, I instantly see what I get; there's no waiting for slides to come back.
- It's easy to change; if I don't like the result, I can easily change it immediately.
- I can easily output what I create in a number of formats: slides, color transparencies, etc.
- Unlike most computer presentation systems, this one gives me random access; once I start a presentation, I can move around if I need to. I can go back to an image in response to a question. I can skip images that I don't need. In short, I have greater control.
- I've been able to use the system anywhere. Since 1987, I've used it in Canada, Japan, Europe, Saudi Arabia, Mexico, Australia, Singapore, Malaysia, and Kuwait.

One note of caution: all VideoShow dealers are not alike, so choose wisely. Some are able to sell you the box, just the way someone would sell you a videocassette recorder. He or she can show you how to hook it up to a TV, how to put in the videotape, but not how to put something on the videotape. Choose your vendor carefully to make sure he or she provides the support you need to get the most from your system. Obviously, this cautionary note applies to any software or hardware you buy.

SUMMARY

VideoShow HQ
General Parametrics Corp.
1250 9th Street
Berkeley, CA 94710
(510) 524-3950
List Price: VideoShow HQ $4999
PictureIt 5.12 software $399
Printmaker (for printing hard copy) $99
Spectra Star Slide Maker $4999
Requires: 384K RAM, graphics card and monitor, DOS 3.0 or later. Hard disk recommended

PicturePaks
Imagecline
401 East Main Street
Richmond, VA 23219
List Price: $195
A collection of business and technical images.

Freelance Plus for Windows
Version 2.01
Lotus Development Corp.
55 Cambridge Parkway
Cambridge, MA 02142
(617) 577-8500
List Price: $369
Requires: 384K RAM, Windows 3.1
Freelance creates all kinds of charts, has a built-in graphics library, allows you to output to a wide variety of devices (not just VideoShow), and has great tools for editing any graphics.

OTHER PACKAGES

I haven't had the opportunity to use these packages as extensively, so my comments are based upon feedback I've had from participants, etc. But at least this gives you a starting point for looking at what's out there that can improve your presentation graphics.

Harvard Graphics

Software Publishing Corp.
1901 Landings Dr., P.O. Box 54983
Santa Clara, CA 95056
(408) 986-8000
List Price: Windows 2.0 $395, DOS 3.0 $595
Requires: 512K RAM, DOS 2.10 or later
As of this writing, Harvard Graphics is still one of the best-selling graphics packages. When I was in Saudi Arabia in 1988, my hosts at Saudia Airlines raved about it. It's easy to use, they said—and it is. I've experimented with the standard formats and found it easy to create the standard charts that might be used in business. It is extremely user-friendly, but it lacks the freeform-graphics capability of Freelance Plus.

Picture Perfect 4.1

Computer Support Corp.
15926 Midway Road
Dallas, TX 75244
(214) 661-8960
List Price: $295
Requires 512K RAM, DOS 1.0 or later
This package is easy to use and produces exceptional output on laser printers. It provides all the common charts and graphs, is menu-driven, and, while it doesn't have a symbols library built in, it can acquire symbols from a companion package called Arts and Letters (list price $395) from the same company. A large number of help screens are available at almost any point in the development of your charts and graphs.

APPENDIX 3

Sources of Inexpensive Training Materials

1. Overhead Projectors
Elmo Overhead Projectors
Resources for Organizations, Inc.
7620 West 78th Street
Edina, MN 55439
(612) 829-1954

2. Marking Pens
Schwan-Stabilo USA, Inc.
403 Dividend Drive
Peachtree City, GA 30269
(404) 487-5512

*3. High-Quality
Transparency Films*
Tersch Products, Inc.
P.O. Box 118
Rogers, MN 55374
(800) 328-2048

Visualon, Inc.
9000 Sweet Valley Drive
Valley View, OH 44125
(216) 328-9000

Arkwright, Inc.
538 Main Street
Fiskeville, RI 02823
(401) 821-1000

CreativColor Film and Markers
(to be used together) for use on
overhead projectors.
**Resources for
Organizations, Inc.**
7620 West 78th Street
Edina, MN 55439
(612) 829-1954

*4. Thermo Copiers for Making
Transparencies*
**3M Corporation—
Visual Products Division**
3M Austin Center
6801 River Place Blvd.
Austin, TX 78126-9000
(512) 984-1800

Tersch Products, Inc.
P.O. Box 118
Rogers, MN 55374
(800) 328-2048

5. Clip Art
Dover Publications, Inc.
180 Varick Street
New York, NY 10014
(212) 255-3755

Dynamic Graphics, Inc.
6000 North Forest Park Drive
Peoria, IL 61614
(309) 688-8800

Cracked, Crazy, and *Mad* magazines are inexpensive sources of clip art. I suggest you purchase them at used-magazine stores.

7. Press Type Letters
E-Z Industries, Inc.
P.O. Box 829
Westminster, MD 21158
(410) 876-2511

7. Letter Graphix & Typesetter
Esselte Letraset
Letraset USA, Inc.
40 Eisenhower Drive
Paramus, NJ 07652
(201) 845-6100

8. Merlin Lettering Machine
Varitronic Systems, Inc.
300 South Highway 1697
Minneapolis, MN 55426
(800) 637-5461

*9. Canon PC-25 Copier,
Desk-top Size*
**International Office
Systems, Inc.**
2741 West 80th Street
Bloomington, MN 55431
(612) 456-9999

10. Learning Instruments
Personal Profile System
Personal Profile Manual
Library of Classical Patterns
Climate Impact Profile
The Job Factor Analysis
Style Analysis
Attitudinal Listening Profile
Values Analysis Profile
Listening Climate Indicator
Personal Matrix
Child's Profile
The Resources Group, Inc.
7620 West 78th Street
Edina, MN 55439
(612) 829-1954

11. Books
Cheers, Smiles, Friends, Happiness, Thanks and Kindness Books, a collection of "Lovable, Liveable, and Laughable Lines" compiled by Marcia and Dave Kaplan. Pictures are by Phil Mendez, a former Disney animator.
**Resources for
Organizations, Inc.**
7620 West 78th Street
Edina, MN 55439
(612) 829-1954

12. Posters
Art 101: Posters, Postcards, Matted Cards, Mounted Prints, Desk Plaques and just about everything else you want in words. These begin with words and then design graphics to reinforce them.
**Resources for
Organizations, Inc.**
7620 West 78th Street
Edina, MN 55439
(612) 829-1954

13. Inexpensive Certificates
The Certificate Gallery
55 King Street
Monson, MA 01057
(800) 423-3459

14. Powerful Presentations
Music
Six types of music in 30 minute blocks, on three audiotapes for use in live presentations with all royalties paid. Music for: Introduction (walk-in); Exit; Breaks; Reflection; Discussion; and Games.
$59.00 (three-tape set)
Resources for Organizations, Inc.
7620 West 70th Street
Edina, MN 55439
(612) 829-1954

APPENDIX   4
Activity Guide Sheets

Here are four activity guide sheets from the *Creative Training Techniques Seminar Workbook* which were referred to in Chapter Two. These can be freely reproduced as long as they're for educational purposes, for which there is no charge. However, I ask that each page carry this notation: Copyright 1989 and 1994, Resources for Organizations, Inc., Robert W. Pike, CSP. Used by permission.

Special permission is required to include in any publications that may be for sale. To do so contact: Resources for Organizations, Inc., 7620 West 78th Street, Edina, MN 55439, (612) 829-1954.

FOUR "FACTS"

Some possible uses of this activity are included on page 124.

Part I   On this sheet, please list four facts about yourself. Three of them should **be** true. One of them should be false.

1.

2.

3.

4.

Part II   Now, as a group, do the following steps, in order, one at a time.

1.   List below the name of each person in your group.

2.   Each person reads their four statements aloud.

3.   As each person reads the four statements, list next to his or her name the number of the statement you think is false about them and why.

4.   Once each person has completed sharing the statements, take one person at a time and have each of the remaining people tell which statement is false and why. Then the person who shared **the four** statements originally can reveal which one was really false.

5.   Do this for each of the people in your group.

1.   Name_____ Statement number _____ is false

       because _____ .

2.   Name_____ Statement number _____ is false

       because _____ .

3.   Name_____ Statement number _____ is false

       because _____ .

4.   Name_____ Statement number _____ is false

       because _____ .

5.   Name_____ Statement number _____ is false

       because _____ .

6.   Name_____ Statement number _____ is false

       because _____ .

FOUR "FACTS"/SAMPLE DISCUSSION SHEET

Group Leader read:

1. Were you surprised at some of the "facts" that people shared? Which? Why?

2. How good were you as a group and individually at picking the false statement? What does this tell you about making assumptions and judgments about people?

3. Were some of the statements made by different people similar? What reasons could you give for this?

4. Were some of the "facts" quite different? What reasons could you give for this?

PENNY EXERCISE

Source:	Bob Pike
Objective:	To build a team
Category:	Team Builder
Audience:	Any
Group Size:	Enough to form participants into teams
Time:	Five to seven minutes
Equipment:	Flip chart and markers or write-on transparency film Some pennies A blank sheet of paper per participant
Note:	At the end, when dealing with participants who think they already know everything there is to know about the subject, point out that we are selective learners and there is always something new to be learned.
Process:	Up in the corner of a blank sheet of paper, ask each participant to write down the numbers of pennies s/he's handled in his/her life. Have some or all (depending on group size) call out the figure they wrote down. Record these figures on flip chart or foil. Ask each to draw two large circles on the piece of paper. Ask them to refrain from taking a penny from their purse or pocket. Have them label one circle "front" and one "back." Ask them to reproduce the front and back of a penny in one minute. Point out how many they've handled. At the end of a minute point out how we can be overly familiar with an object or situation or event and not really see it. Expand on this. To learn the value of a team, ask them to go around the team and each person in turn gives one thing they have on their drawing. As each gives a feature, the others add the feature to their own drawings, so that each one's "picture" becomes more and more complete through shared knowledge. Discuss value of team in open-forum. Tell them they can now look at a penny. Allow time for them to do so and to comment to each other. Tell them the Treasury Department estimates we handle 1,000 pennies per year. Refer back to their estimates. Many will be over 100,000. Some may be over 1,000,000. (Considering their ages, they look MAH-VEL-OUS.)

ALPHABET SEARCH

Source: Southwestern Bell Telephone, Atlanta, GA CTT

Objective: Team builder
Afternoon energizer
Wholesome competition exercise

Category: Team Builder

Audience: Any

Group Size: Fifteen or more
Teams of five – three or more teams

Time: Fifteen minutes

Equipment: Either one shopping bag or one ice cream bucket per team

Process: Each team is to fill the sack or bucket with objects from individual's pockets, purses, briefcases, etc. One object for each letter of the alphabet: "C" might be credit card, "J" might be jewelry, "L" might be lipstick, "P" might be prescription, etc.

One team member is to be the recorder and list each item as it is put in the container. This is a timed exercise; no team begins until the trainer says go.

The first team to complete the body search, and come up with the 26 items "wins." All other teams continue, however, as the trainer and the recorder check each letter of the alphabet against an item in the sack/bucket. When a winner is established, the teams are told to leave all items as they are. Prizes are given to the winning teams (candy, usually).

The containers are emptied with each person keeping his/her contributions in a pile at his/her place.

Discussion starters:
Are you amazed at what people carry? The diversity? Could the sack/bucket have been filled without the contribution of each team member? Value of teams? Contribution of recorder?

Variation: If the trainer has had the recorder write down the letters of the alphabet vertically down a sheet of paper, then the "process" is not up for discussion.

If the trainer has not given "process," but just said, "Keep track of what you put in the sack and match it to an alphabet letter," then the teams can also discuss how they arrived at their process.

UNIQUENESSES AND COMMONALITIES

Each group of five to seven is given a sheet of flip chart paper and several magic markers, preferably water based, such as Mr. Sketch™. Each group is instructed to draw a circle and to put the name of each participant on the outside of the circle. The group is then to do a five minute interview looking for two things: 1. At least two things that are unique about each person; that is, they are the only person in the group that it is true for. 2. At least three to five things that the group has in common, that is true for everybody in the group. Go for the unusual things. A common thing would be that we are all in this group, we are all in this room, we are all at this meeting, etc. Those are boring. What we want to be is unusual, like everybody in this group is a chocoholic, everybody in the group has at least one brother and one sister, etc. The groups have five to seven minutes to do this. They then have three minutes to pick a name for their group and add that and also to identify the most unusual thing about one person and the most unusual thing about the group that they have in common. Do several rounds going from table to table and sharing the most unique thing about one person and then go back around with the most unique thing the group has in common.

APPENDIX 5

Overhead Transparencies

PIKE'S LAWS OF ADULT LEARNING

Here are some visuals that represent the key concepts of the book. I've given them to you in two forms. The first form occupies a full page, which you may want to remove, add some color, and frame as a reminder. The second is a pocket-sized card that can be removed and easily carried.

The larger size also can be enlarged on a copy machine and used to make a transparency. My only requirement, again, is that each transparency carry this notation: Copyright 1989 and 1994, Resources for Organizations, Inc., Robert W. Pike, CSP. Used by permission.

PIKE'S FIRST LAW

Adults are babies with big bodies.

PIKE'S SECOND LAW

People don't argue with their own data.

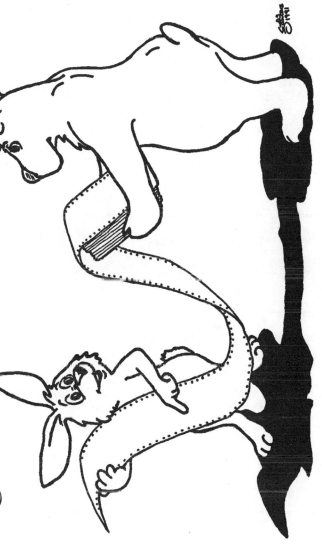

PIKE'S THIRD LAW

Learning is directly
proportional to the
amount of fun
you have.

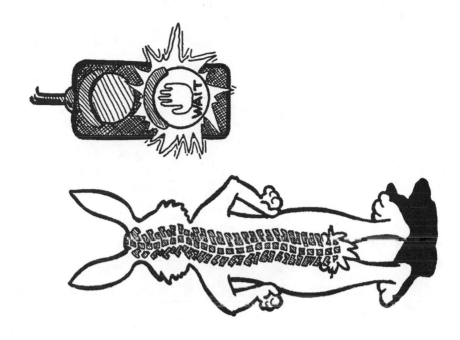

PIKE'S FOURTH LAW

Learning has not taken place until behavior has changed.

PIKE'S FIFTH LAW

Fu Yu
Wu Yu
Wzu Tu Yu

TRANSLATION:

Mama's havin' it
and Papa's havin' it
ain't like baby havin' it.

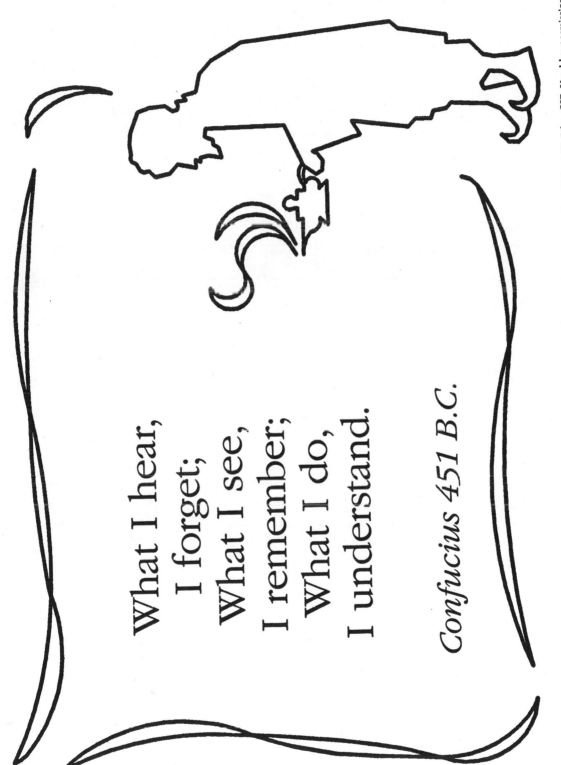

What I hear,
I forget;
What I see,
I remember;
What I do,
I understand.

Confucius 451 B.C.

Five Levels of Competence

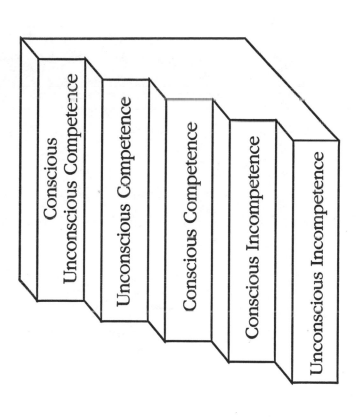

- Conscious Unconscious Competence
- Unconscious Competence
- Conscious Competence
- Conscious Incompetence
- Unconscious Incompetence

adapted from William Howell

A man with an experience
is never at the mercy of a man
with an argument.

C. S. Lewis

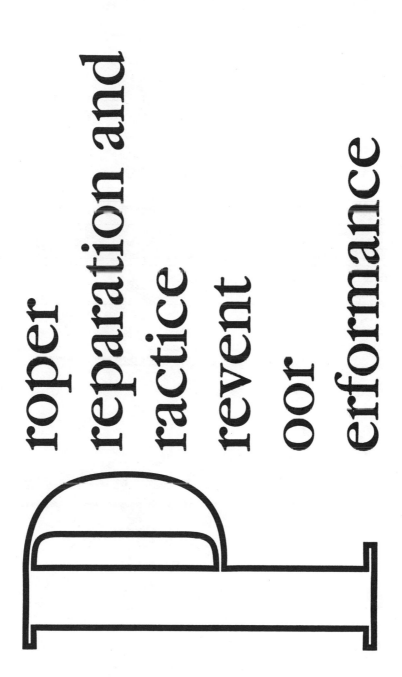

roper

reparation and

ractice

revent

oor

erformance

Radio Station WII-FM:
What's In It For Me?

Radio Station MMFI-AM:
Make Me Feel Important About Myself

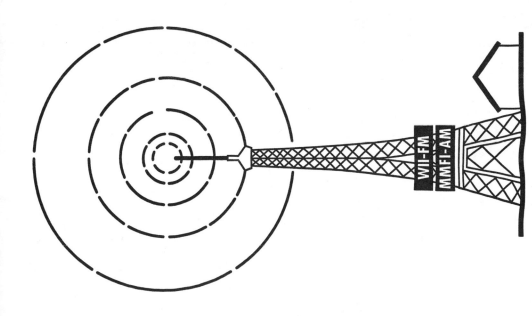

PIKE'S RULE OF
CLEAR INSTRUCTIONS

If in doubt, spell it out!
(in writing!)

Basic Principles of Motivation

1. You cannot motivate other people.

2. All people are motivated.

3. People do things for their reasons,
   NOT your reasons.

4. A person's strength OVEREXTENDED
   can become that person's weakness.

PIKE'S RULE
OF INSTRUCTIONAL EXCELLENCE

Have the *attitude*
of a *learner:*

The greatest need of every human being is the need for APPRECIATION.

adapted from William James

How We Receive Information

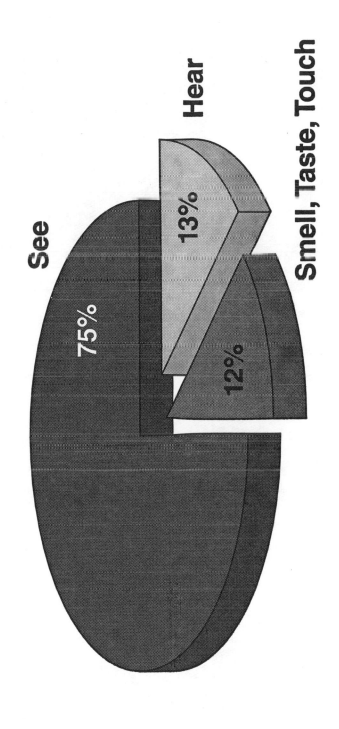

See — 75%

Hear — 13%

Smell, Taste, Touch — 12%

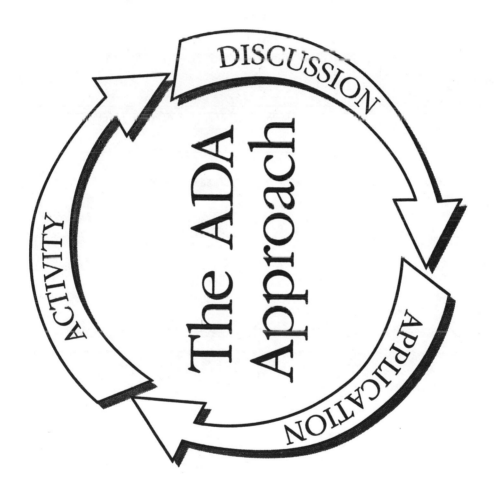

The ADA Approach

DISCUSSION
APPLICATION
ACTIVITY

Presentation Outline

A. History of the Problem

B. Current Condition of the Problem

C. Possible Solutions

D. Analysis of Solutions

E. Best Solution & Why

F. Call to Action

Presentation Outline

A. Problem

B. Solution

C. Call to Action

Presentation Outline

A. Past

B. Present

C. Future

Presentation Outline

NEW-TWIST APPROACH

A. An old idea

B. A new twist

C. How you found it

D. How it worked

E. How listeners can use it

F. How they can start

G. Call to action

INDEX

WANT MORE COPIES?

This and most other Lakewood books are available at special quantity discounts when purchased in bulk. For details write: Lakewood Books, 50 South Ninth Street, Minneapolis, MN 55402. Or call (800) 707-7769, (612) 333-0471.

OTHER LAKEWOOD PRODUCTS

The Best of Creative Training Techniques Newsletter $24.95

The Best of TRAINING $59.95

Powerful Audiovisual Techniques: 101 Ideas to Increase
    the Impact and Effectiveness of Your Training $14.95

Motivating Your Trainees: 101 Proven Ways to Get Them
    to Really Want to Learn $14.95

Managing the Front-End of Training: 101 Ways to Analyze
    Training Needs—And Get Results! $14.95

Dynamic Openers & Energizers: 101 Tips and Tactics
    for Enlivening Your Training Classroom $14.95

Optimizing Training Transfer: 101 Techniques for Improving
    Training Retention and Application $14.95

101 Games for Trainers: A Collection of the Best Activities
    from Creative Training Techniques Newsletter $21.95

101 More Games for Trainers: A Collection of the Best Activities
    from Creative Training Techniques Newsletter $21.95

Dave Arch's ALL NEW Tricks for Trainers: 57 Tricks and Techniques
    to Grab and Hold the Attention of Any Audience $24.95

Creative Training Techniques Newsletter
    (12 issues per year) $109.00

TRAINING Magazine $79.00

"Born to Train" T-Shirt
    Red, white and blue on black. Available only in Large and X-Large $12.00

TO ORDER CONTACT: Lakewood Books, 50 South Ninth Street, Minneapolis, MN 55402. Or call (800) 707-7769, (612) 333-0471. Fax orders to (612) 340-4819. Visit our web site at www.trainingsupersite.com

UNCONDITIONAL GUARANTEE

Examine and use any of the resources on this page for a full 30 days. If you are not completely satisfied, for any reason whatsoever, simply return them and receive a full refund of the purchase price.

PIKE'S FIRST LAW

Adults are babies
with big bodies.

PIKE'S SECOND LAW

People don't argue
with their own data.

PIKE'S THIRD LAW

Learning is directly
proportional to the
amount of fun you have.

PIKE'S FOURTH LAW

Learning has not taken place
until behavior has changed.

PIKE'S FIFTH LAW

Fu Yu
Wu Yu
Wzu Tu Yu

TRANSLATION:

Mama's havin' it
and Papa's havin' it
ain't like baby havin' it.

What I hear, I forget;
What I see, I remember;
What I do, I understand.

Confucius 451 B.C.

Five Levels of Competence

*adapted from
William Howell*

A man with an experience
is never at the mercy of a man
with an argument.

C. S. Lewis

6 P's of Preparation

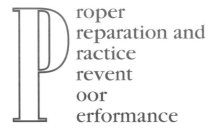

Proper
reparation and
ractice
revent
oor
erformance

PIKE'S RULE OF INSTRUCTIONAL EXCELLENCE

Have the attitude of a learner.

Radio Station WII-FM:
What's In It For Me?

Radio Station MMFI-AM:
Make Me Feel Important
About Myself

The greatest need of every human
being is the need for
APPRECIATION.

adapted from William James

PIKE'S RULE OF CLEAR INSTRUCTIONS

If in doubt, spell it out!
(in writing!)

How We Receive Information

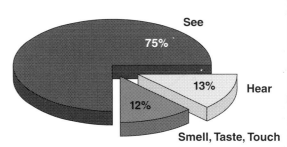

See 75%
Hear 13%
Smell, Taste, Touch 12%

Basic Principles of Motivation

1. You cannot motivate other people.
2. All people are motivated.
3. People do things for their reasons, NOT your reasons.
4. A person's strength OVEREXTENDED can become that person's weakness.

ACTIVITY
DISCUSSION
APPLICATION

The ADA Approach